Also by John Crowe Ransom

Poems and Essays
Two Gentlemen in Bonds
Chills and Fever

Selected Poems

Third Edition, Revised and Enlarged

John Crowe Ransom

Selected Poems

Alfred A. Knopf   New York   1991

THIS IS A BORZOI BOOK
PUBLISHED BY ALFRED A. KNOPF, INC.

Copyright 1924, 1927, 1934, 1939, 1945,
© 1962, 1963, 1969 by Alfred A. Knopf, Inc.
Copyright renewed 1952, 1954 by John Crowe Ransom
All rights reserved under International and Pan-American Copyright Conventions.
Published in the United States by Alfred A. Knopf, Inc., New York,
and simultaneously in Canada by Random House of Canada Limited, Toronto.
Distributed by Random House, Inc., New York.

Library of Congress Cataloging-in-Publication Data
Ransom, John Crowe, 1888–1974.
[Poems. Selections]
Selected poems / by John Crowe Ransom.—3rd ed.
p.   cm.
"A Borzoi book"—T.p. verso.
ISBN 0–679–40257–8
I. Title.
PS3535.A635A6   1991
811'.52–dc20   90–52904   CIP

Published June 1945.
Reprinted one time
Second edition revised, enlarged, reset, and printed
from new plates, June 1963.
Reprinted two times
Third edition newly revised, enlarged, reset, and
printed from new plates, July 1969.
Fifth printing, June 1991
Manufactured in the United States of America

Contents

The Innocent Doves

The Manliness of Men

Two Gentlemen in Bonds
(*in twelve sonnets*)

Sixteen Poems in Eight Pairings

(with original and final versions studied comparatively)

The Innocent Doves

Miriam Tazewell

When Miriam Tazewell heard the tempest bursting
And his wrathy whips across the sky drawn crackling
She stuffed her ears for fright like a young thing
And with heart full of the flowers took to weeping.

But the earth shook dry his old back in good season,
He had weathered storms that drenched him deep as this one,
And the sun, Miriam, ascended to his dominion,
The storm was withered against his empyrean.

After the storm she went forth with skirts kilted
To see in the hot sun her lawn deflowered,
Her tulip, iris, peony strung and pelted,
Pots of geranium spilled and the stalks naked.

The spring transpired in that year with no flowers
But the regular stars went busily on their courses,
Suppers and cards were calendared, and some bridals,
And the birds demurely sang in the bitten poplars.

To Miriam Tazewell the whole world was villain,
The principle of the beast was low and masculine,
And not to unstop her own storm and be maudlin,
For weeks she went untidy, she went sullen.

Spectral Lovers

By night they haunted a thicket of April mist,
Out of that black ground suddenly come to birth,
Else angels lost in each other and fallen on earth.
Lovers they knew they were, but why unclasped, unkissed?
Why should two lovers be frozen apart in fear?
And yet they were, they were.

Over the shredding of an April blossom
Scarcely her fingers touched him, quick with care,
Yet of evasions even she made a snare.
The heart was bold that clanged within her bosom,
The moment perfect, the time stopped for them,
Still her face turned from him.

Strong were the batteries of the April night
And the stealthy emanations of the field;
Should the walls of her prison undefended yield
And open her treasure to the first clamorous knight?
"This is the mad moon, and shall I surrender all?
If he but ask it I shall."

And gesturing largely to the moon of Easter,
Mincing his steps and swishing the jubilant grass,
Beheading some field-flowers that had come to pass,
He had reduced his tributaries faster
Had not considerations pinched his heart
Unfitly for his art.

"Do I reel with the sap of April like a drunkard?
Blessed is he that taketh this richest of cities;
But it is so stainless the sack were a thousand pities.
This is that marble fortress not to be conquered,
Lest its white peace in the black flame turn to tinder
And an unutterable cinder."

4

They passed me once in April, in the mist.
No other season is it when one walks and discovers
Two tall and wandering, like spectral lovers,
White in the season's moon-gold and amethyst,
Who touch quick fingers fluttering like a bird
Whose songs shall never be heard.

The Rose

I entered weary of my woes
The room in which I was to sit
With dreary unbelieving books,
Astonished, as you may suppose,
To find such happy change in it:
There stood a most celestial rose
And looked the flower that my love looks
When men are mad to seek that face
Whose smile is very Heaven's grace.

I blessed the heart that wished me well
When I had been bereft of much,
And brought such word of beauty back;
I went like one escaping hell
To drink the fragrance and to touch,
And stroked, O ludicrous to tell,
A horrid thing of bric-a-brac,
A make-believe and mockery
And nothing that a rose must be.

Red real roses keep a thorn
To save their sweetness for a while
And in their perfect date unfold,
But you beyond all women born
Have spent so easily your smile
That I am not the less forlorn
Nor these ironic walls less cold
Because it smiles, the heartless rose,
As you are smiling, I suppose.

Bells for John Whiteside's Daughter

There was such speed in her little body,
And such lightness in her footfall,
It is no wonder her brown study
Astonishes us all.

Her wars were bruited in our high window.
We looked among orchard trees and beyond
Where she took arms against her shadow,
Or harried unto the pond

The lazy geese, like a snow cloud
Dripping their snow on the green grass,
Tricking and stopping, sleepy and proud,
Who cried in goose, Alas,

For the tireless heart within the little
Lady with rod that made them rise
From their noon apple-dreams and scuttle
Goose-fashion under the skies!

But now go the bells, and we are ready,
In one house we are sternly stopped
To say we are vexed at her brown study,
Lying so primly propped.

The Tall Girl

The Queens of Hell had lissome necks to crane
At the tall girl approaching with long tread
And, when she was caught up even with them, nodded:
"If the young miss with gold hair might not disdain,
We would esteem her company over the plain,
To profit us all where the dogs will be out barking,
And we'll go by the windows where the young men are working
And tomorrow we will all come home again."

But the Queen of Heaven on the other side of the road
In the likeness, I hear, of a plain motherly woman
Made a wry face, despite it was so common
To be worsted by the smooth ladies of Hell,
And crisped her sweet tongue: "This never will come to good!
Just an old woman, my pet, that wishes you well."

Piazza Piece

—I am a gentleman in a dustcoat trying
To make you hear. Your ears are soft and small
And listen to an old man not at all,
They want the young men's whispering and sighing.
But see the roses on your trellis dying
And hear the spectral singing of the moon;
For I must have my lovely lady soon,
I am a gentleman in a dustcoat trying.

—I am a lady young in beauty waiting
Until my truelove comes, and then we kiss.
But what grey man among the vines is this
Whose words are dry and faint as in a dream?
Back from my trellis, Sir, before I scream!
I am a lady young in beauty waiting.

Lady Lost

This morning, flew up the lane
A timid lady bird to our birdbath
And eyed her image dolefully as death;
This afternoon, knocked on our windowpane
To be let in from the rain.

And when I caught her eye
She looked aside, but at the clapping thunder
And sight of the whole world blazing up like tinder
Looked in on us again so miserably
It was as if she would cry.

So I will go out into the park and say,
"Who has lost a delicate brown-eyed lady
In the West End section? Or has anybody
Injured some fine woman in some dark way
Last night, or yesterday?

"Let the owner come and claim possession,
No questions will be asked. But stroke her gently
With loving words, and she will evidently
Return to her full soft-haired white-breasted fashion
And her right home and her right passion."

Blue Girls

Twirling your blue skirts, travelling the sward
Under the towers of your seminary,
Go listen to your teachers old and contrary
Without believing a word.

Tie the white fillets then about your hair
And think no more of what will come to pass
Than bluebirds that go walking on the grass
And chattering on the air.

Practise your beauty, blue girls, before it fail;
And I will cry with my loud lips and publish
Beauty which all our power shall never establish,
It is so frail.

For I could tell you a story which is true;
I know a woman with a terrible tongue,
Blear eyes fallen from blue,
All her perfections tarnished—yet it is not long
Since she was lovelier than any of you.

Janet Waking

Beautifully Janet slept
Till it was deeply morning. She woke then
And thought about her dainty-feathered hen,
To see how it had kept.

One kiss she gave her mother.
Only a small one gave she to her daddy
Who would have kissed each curl of his shining baby;
No kiss at all for her brother.

"Old Chucky, old Chucky!" she cried,
Running across the world upon the grass
To Chucky's house, and listening. But alas,
Her Chucky had died.

It was a transmogrifying bee
Came droning down on Chucky's old bald head
And sat and put the poison. It scarcely bled,
But how exceedingly

And purply did the knot
Swell with the venom and communicate
Its rigor! Now the poor comb stood up straight
But Chucky did not.

So there was Janet
Kneeling on the wet grass, crying her brown hen
(Translated far beyond the daughters of men)
To rise and walk upon it.

And weeping fast as she had breath
Janet implored us, "Wake her from her sleep!"
And would not be instructed in how deep
Was the forgetful kingdom of death.

Eclogue

JANE SNEED BEGAN IT: My poor John, alas,
Ten years ago, pretty it was in a ring
To run as boys and girls do in the grass—
At that time leap and hollo and skip and sing
Came easily to pass.

JOHN BLACK SAID: I'll interpret what you mean.
Our infant selves played happily with our others,
The cunning me and mine came not between
Which like a sword is, O sweethearts and brothers
Numberless, who have seen.

JANE SNEED: I tell you what I used to do.
For joy I used to run by river or wood
To see with what speed all came trooping too;
Those days I could not quit you if I would,
Nor yet quit me could you.

JOHN BLACK RETURNED: But now, Jane, it appears
We are sly travelers, keeping good lookout
Against the face whose ravage cries for tears;
Old friends, ill met; and supposing I call out,
"Draw nigh, friend of those years"—

Before he think of any reason why,
The features of that man resolve and burn
For one long look—but then the flame must die.
The cold hearts in us mortally return,
We must not fructify.

JANE SNEED SAID BITTERLY: Why, John, you are right.
We were spendthrifts of joy when we were young,
But we became usurious, and in fright

Conceived that such a waste of days was wrong
For marchers unto night.

JOHN BLACK SAID: Yes, exactly, that was when
It happened. For Time involved us: in his toils
We learned to fear. And every day since then
We are mortals teasing for immortal spoils,
Desperate women and men.

JANE SNEED CONSENTED: It was nothing but this.
Love suffereth long, is kind—but not in fear.
For boys run banded, and simple sweethearts kiss,
Till in one day the dream of Death appear—
Then metamorphosis.

JOHN BLACK SAID: To explain mistrust and wars,
Theogony has a black witch with hell's broth;
Or a preposterous marriage of fleshless stars;
Or the Fiend's own naked person; or God wroth
Fingering his red scars.

And philosophy, an art of equal worth,
Tells of a flaw in the firmament—spots in the sun—
A Third Day's error when the upheaving earth
Was young and prime—a Fate reposed upon
The born before their birth.

JANE SNEED WITH GRIM LIPS MOCKED HIM: Who can tell—
Not I, not you—about those mysteries!
Something, John Black, came flapping out of hell
And wrought between us, and the chasm is
Digged, and it digged it well.

JOHN BLACK IN DEPRECATION SAID: Be sure
That love has suffered a most fatal eclipse;
All brotherhoods, filialities insecure;
Lovers compounding honey on their lips
With deep doubts to endure.

JANE SNEED SIGHED SLOWLY: I suppose it stands
Just so. Yet I can picture happiness—
Perhaps there wander lovers in some lands
Who when Night comes, when it is fathomless,
Consort their little hands;

And well, John Black, the darkened lovers may,
The hands hold much of heat in little storage,
The eyes are almost torches good as day,
And one flame to the other flame cries Courage,
When heart to heart slide they;

JOHN BLACK'S THE LAST SAY THEN: O innocent dove,
This is a dream. We lovers mournfully
Exchange our bleak despairs. We are one part love
And nine parts bitter thought. As well might be
Beneath ground as above.

Vaunting Oak

He is a tower unleaning. But how he'll break
If Heaven assault him with full wind and sleet,
And what uproar tall trees concumbent make!

More than a hundred years and a hundred feet
Naked he rears against cold skies eruptive,
Only his temporal twigs unsure of seat,

And the frail leaves of a season, who are susceptive
To the mad humors of wind, and turn and flee
In panic round the stem on which they are captive.

Now a certain heart, too young and mortally
Yoked with an unbeliever of bantering brood,
Observed, as an eminent witness of life, the tree;

She exulted, wrapped in a phantasy of good:
"Be the great oak for his long winterings
Our symbol of love, better than summer's brood!"

Then the patient oak, delivered of his pangs,
Put forth profuse his green banners of peace
And testified to her with innumerable tongues.

And what but she fetch me up to the steep place
Where the oak vaunted? A flat where birdsong flew
Had to be traversed, and a quick populace

Of daisies and yellow kinds, and here she knew,
Instructed well by much mortality,
Better than brag in this distraught purlieu.

Above their pied and dusty clumps was he
Standing, sheer on his hill, not much soiled over
By the knobs and broken boughs of an old tree.

She looked and murmured, "Established there, forever!"
But, that her pitiful error be undone,
I knocked upon his house, a sorrowing lover,

And like a funeral came the hollow tone.
"The grand old fellow," I grieved, "holds gallantly,
But before our joy has lapsed, even, will be gone."

I beat more sternly, and the dolorous cry
Boomed till its loud reverberance outsounded
The singing of bees; or the coward birds that fly

Otherwhere with their songs when summer is sped,
And if they stayed would perish miserably;
Or the weeping girl remembering her dread.

Two in August

Two that could not have lived their single lives
As can some husbands and wives
Did something strange: they tensed their vocal cords
And attacked each other with silences and words
Like catapulted stones and arrowed knives.

Dawn was not yet; night is for loving or sleeping,
Sweet dreams or safekeeping;
Yet he of the wide brows that were used to laurel
And she, the famed for gentleness, must quarrel.
Furious both of them, and scared, and weeping.

How sleepers groan, twitch, wake to such a mood
Is not well understood,
Nor why two entities grown almost one
Should rend and murder trying to get undone,
With individual tigers in their blood.

She in terror fled from the marriage chamber
Circuiting the dark rooms like a string of amber
Round and round and back,
And would not light one lamp against the black,
And heard the clock that clanged: Remember, Remember.

And he must tread barefooted the dim lawn,
Soon he was up and gone;
High in the trees the night-mastered birds were crying
With fear upon their tongues, no singing nor flying
Which are their lovely attitudes by dawn.

Whether those bird-cries were of heaven or hell
There is no way to tell;
In the long ditch of darkness the man walked
Under the hackberry trees where the birds talked
With words too sad and strange to syllable.

Emily Hardcastle, Spinster

We shall come tomorrow morning, who were not to have her love,
We shall bring no face of envy but a gift of praise and lilies
To the stately ceremonial we are not the heroes of.

Let the sisters now attend her, who are red-eyed, who are wroth;
They were younger, she was finer, for they wearied of the waiting
And they married them to merchants, being unbelievers both.

I was dapper when I dangled in my pepper-and-salt;
We were only local beauties, and we beautifully trusted
If the proud one had to tarry, one would have her by default.

But right across the threshold has her grizzled Baron come;
Let them robe her, Bride and Princess, who'll go down a leafy archway
And seal her to the Stranger for his castle in the gloom.

Moments of Minnie

We must not honor a girl of Minnie's kind
Whose charms are more endearing than her mind,
If we are the casuists we think we are,
Yet it oppressed me when an evil star
Had thralled so lazy and beautiful a creature
And scarred and misshapen her most tender feature.

Mouth-corners were pulled down, and the outleaning
Of her soft lips drew back their gallant meaning.
Pain is hideous; it pinched the vaulted line
To a flatness terrible, yet no doing of mine.
And pain is primitive; it undid words
And left her no more speech than tuneless birds.
She uttered and I heard that which could not
Be foreseen, nor yet afterward forgot:
Oh, Oh, Oh! not a word, and not a name,
And no tears flowed, yet wry and dry it came
Till I trembled, and I fled, I had to find
Distance for a contagion-catching mind.

I wash my mind of those old memories.
Better now to reconstitute the trees
And the bridegroom scarlet bird of April crying
To his brown one embowered; then the flying
Mirth that bubbled off this woman's mouth
From secret wells abundant as the South
Which spilled their joy too thickly to be speech.
Ah, Ah, Ah! she murmured deeply, and each
Breath was a new Ah! and I had heard
What never issues on a lettered word.

Somewhere Is Such a Kingdom

The famous kingdom of the birds
Has a sweet tongue and liquid words,
The red-birds polish their notes
In their easy practised throats.
Smooth as orators are the thrushes
Of the airy city of the bushes,
And God reward the fierce cock wrens
Who have such suavity with their hens.

To me this has its worth
As I sit upon the earth
Lacking my winter and quiet hearth.
For I go up into a nook
With a mind burdened or a book,
And hear no strife nor quarreling
As the birds and their wives sing.

Or, so it has been today.
Yet I cannot therefore say
If the red-bird, wren, or thrush
Know when to speak and when to hush;
Though their manifest education
Be a right enunciation,
And their chief excellence
A verbal elegance.
I cannot say if the wind never blows,
Nor how it sometimes goes.

This I know, that if they wrangle,
Their words inevitably will jangle.
If they be hateful as men
They will be harsh as we have been.
When they go to pecking

You will soon hear shrieking,
And they who will have the law,
How those will jaw!
Girls that have unlawful dreams
Will waken full of their own screams,
And boys that get too arrant
Will have rows with a parent,—
And when friend falls out with friend
All songs must have quick end.

Have they not claws like knives?
Have not these gentlemen wives?

But when they croak and fleer and swear,
My dull heart I must take elsewhere;
For I will see if God has made
Otherwhere another shade
Where the men or beasts or birds
Exchange few words and pleasant words.
And dare I think it is absurd
If no such beast were, no such bird?

Parting at Dawn

If there was a broken whispering by night
It was an image of the coward heart,
But the white dawn assures them how to part—
Stoics are born on the cold glitter of light
And with the morning star lovers take flight.
Say then your parting; and most dry should you drain
Your lips of the wine, your eyes of the frantic rain,
Till these be as the barren anchorite.

And then? O dear Sir, stumbling down the street,
Continue, till you come to wars and wounds;
Beat the air, Madam, till your house-clock sounds;
And if no Lethe flows beneath your casement,
And when ten years have not brought full effacement,
Philosophy was wrong, and you may meet.

Good Ships

Fleet ships encountering on the high seas
Who speak, and then unto the vast diverge,
Two hailed each other, poised on the loud surge
Of one of Mrs. Grundy's Tuesday teas,
Nor trimmed one sail to baffle the driving breeze.
A macaroon absorbed all her emotion;
His hue was ruddy but an effect of ocean;
They exchanged the nautical technicalities.

It was only a nothing or so until they parted.
Away they went, most certainly bound for port,
So seaworthy one felt they could not sink;
Still there was a tremor shook them, I should think,
Beautiful timbers fit for storm and sport
And unto miserly merchant hulks converted.

Romance of a Youngest Daughter

Who will wed the Dowager's youngest daughter,
The Captain? filled with ale?
He moored his expected boat to a stake in the water
And stumbled on sea-legs into the Hall for mating,
Only to be seduced by her lady-in-waiting,
Round-bosomed, and not so pale.

Or the thrifty burgher in boots and fancy vest
With considered views of marriage?
By the tidy scullery maid he was impressed
Who kept that house from depreciation and dirt,
But wife does double duty and takes no hurt,
So he rode her home in his carriage.

Never the spare young scholar antiquary
Who was their next resort;
They let him wait in the crypt of the Old Library
And found him compromised with a Saxon book,
Claiming his truelove Learning kept that nook
And promised sweet disport.

Desirée (of a mother's christening) never shall wed
Though fairest child of her womb;
"We will have revenge," her injured Ladyship said,
"Henceforth the tightest nunnery be thy bed
By the topmost stair! When the ill-bred lovers come
We'll say, She is not at home."

Vision by Sweetwater

Go and ask Robin to bring the girls over
To Sweetwater, said my Aunt; and that was why
It was like a dream of ladies sweeping by
The willows, clouds, deep meadowgrass, and river.

Robin's sisters and my Aunt's lily daughter
Laughed and talked, and tinkled light as wrens
If there were a little colony all hens
To go walking by the steep turn of Sweetwater.

Let them alone, dear Aunt, just for one minute
Till I go fishing in the dark of my mind:
Where have I seen before, against the wind,
These bright virgins, robed and bare of bonnet,

Flowing with music of their strange quick tongue
And adventuring with delicate paces by the stream,—
Myself a child, old suddenly at the scream
From one of the white throats which it hid among?

April Treason

So he took her as anointed
In the part he had appointed,
She was lips for smiling faintly,
Eyes to look and level quaintly,
Length of limb and splendors of the bust
Which he honored as he must.

Queen of women playing model,
Pure of brow but brain not idle,
Sitting in her silence meetly,
Let her adjective be stately;
So he thought his art would manage right
In the honest Northern light.

But he fashioned it too coldly,
April broke-and-entered boldly,
Thinking how to suit the season's
Odor, savor, heats and treasons:
Painter! do not stoop and play the host
Lest the man come uppermost.

Yet he knew that he was altered
When the perfect woman faltered,
Languish in her softly speaking,
Anguish, even, in her looking:
All the art had fled his fingertips
So he bent and kissed her lips.

He and Venus took their pleasure,
Then he turned upon his treasure,
Took and trampled it with loathing,
Flung it over cliffs to nothing;
Glittering in the sunlight while it fell
Like a lovely shattered shell.

Strict the silence that came onward
As they trod the foothill downward,
One more mocking noon of April,
Mischief always is in April;
Still she touched his fingers cold as ice
And recited, "It was nice."

Judith of Bethulia

Beautiful as the flying legend of some leopard
She had not chosen yet her captain, nor Prince
Depositary to her flesh, and our defense;
A wandering beauty is a blade out of its scabbard.
You know how dangerous, gentlemen of threescore?
May you know it yet ten more.

Nor by process of veiling she grew less fabulous.
Grey or blue veils, we were desperate to study
The invincible emanations of her white body,
And the winds at her ordered raiment were ominous.
Might she walk in the market, sit in the council of soldiers?
Only of the extreme elders.

But a rare chance was the girl's then, when the Invader
Trumpeted from the South, and rumbled from the North,
Beleaguered the city from four quarters of the earth,
Our soldiery too craven and sick to aid her—
Where were the arms could countervail this horde?
Her beauty was the sword.

She sat with the elders, and proved on their blear visage
How bright was the weapon unrusted in her keeping,
While he lay surfeiting on their harvest heaping
Wasting the husbandry of their rarest vintage—
And dreaming of the broad-breasted dames for concubine?
These floated on his wine.

He was lapped with bay-leaves, and grass and fumiter weed,
And from under the wine-film encountered his mortal vision,
For even within his tent she accomplished his derision,
Loosing one veil and another, she stood unafraid;
So he perished. Nor brushed her with even so much as a daisy?
She found his destruction easy.

The heathen have all perished. The victory was furnished.
We smote them hiding in vineyards, barns, annexes,
And now their white bones clutter the holes of foxes,
And the chieftain's head, with grinning sockets, and varnished—
Is it hung on the sky with a hideous epitaphy?
No, the woman keeps the trophy.

May God send unto our virtuous lady her Prince!
It is stated she went reluctant to that orgy,
Yet a madness fevers our young men, and not the clergy
Nor the elders have turned them unto modesty since.
Inflamed by the thought of her nakedness with desire?
Yes, and chilled with fear and despair.

Her Eyes

To a woman that I knew
Were eyes of an extravagant hue,
They were china blue.

Those I wear upon my head
Are sometimes green and sometimes red,
I said.

My mother's eyes are wet and blear,
My little sister's are not clear,
Poor silly dear.

It must be given to but few,
A pair of eyes so utter blue
And new;

Where does she keep them from this glare
Of the monstrous sun and the wind's flare
Without any wear,

And were they never in the night
Stricken by artificial light
Much too bright,

And had the splendid beast no heart
That boiled with tears and baked with smart
The ocular part?

I'll have no business with those eyes,
They are not kind, they are not wise,
They are two great lies.

A woman shooting such blue flame
I apprehend will get some blame
On her good name.

Parting, without a Sequel

She has finished and sealed the letter
At last, which he so richly has deserved,
With characters venomous and hatefully curved,
And nothing could be better.

But even as she gave it
Saying to the blue-capped functioner of doom,
"Into his hands," she hoped the leering groom
Might somewhere lose and leave it.

Then all the blood
Forsook the face. She was too pale for tears,
Observing the ruin of her younger years.
She went and stood

Under her father's vaunting oak
Who kept his peace in wind and sun, and glistened
Stoical in the rain; to whom she listened
If he spoke.

And now the agitation of the rain
Rasped his sere leaves, and he talked low and gentle
Reproaching the wan daughter by the lintel;
Ceasing and beginning again.

Away went the messenger's bicycle,
His serpent's track went up the hill forever,
And all the time she stood there hot as fever
And cold as any icicle.

Hilda

The dearest was the one to whom it fell
To walk and wear her beauty as in a play
To be enacted nobly on a great day;
And stormily we approved the bosom-swell,
And the tones tinkling. For her touch and smell
I brought bright flowers, till garlanded she stood
Scared with her splendor, as in the sight of God
A pale girl curtsying with an asphodel.

No, No, she answered in the extreme of fear,
I cannot. On the dropping of those petals
Rode the Estranger, scorning their sweet mettles,
Blossoms and woman too; him she looked at,
Not me who praised; she was too honest for that,
I was a clod mumbling, to catch her ear.

I I

The perished were the fairest. And now uprise
Particular ghosts, who hollow and clamorous
Come as blanched lepers crying, "Do not spurn us,"
Ringing in my ears, wetting my eyes,
Obsequious phantoms and disbodied sighs.
Soon they are frightened and go fast; a smoke
Which clung about my quincebushes, then broke,
And while I look is smeared upon the skies.

But Hilda! proudest, lingering last alone,
Wreathing my roses with blue bitter dust,
Think not I would reject you, for I must
Weep for your nakedness and no retinue,
And leap up as of old to follow you;
But what I wear is flesh; it weighs like stone.

34

The Manliness of Men

Winter Remembered

Two evils, monstrous either one apart,
Possessed me, and were long and loath at going:
A cry of Absence, Absence, in the heart,
And in the wood the furious winter blowing.

Think not, when fire was bright upon my bricks,
And past the tight boards hardly a wind could enter,
I glowed like them, the simple burning sticks,
Far from my cause, my proper heat and center.

Better to walk forth in the frozen air
And wash my wound in the snows; that would be healing;
Because my heart would throb less painful there,
Being caked with cold, and past the smart of feeling.

And where I walked, the murderous winter blast
Would have this body bowed, these eyeballs streaming,
And though I think this heart's blood froze not fast
It ran too small to spare one drop for dreaming.

Dear love, these fingers that had known your touch,
And tied our separate forces first together,
Were ten poor idiot fingers not worth much,
Ten frozen parsnips hanging in the weather.

Dead Boy

The little cousin is dead, by foul subtraction,
A green bough from Virginia's aged tree,
And none of the county kin like the transaction,
Nor some of the world of outer dark, like me.

A boy not beautiful, nor good, nor clever,
A black cloud full of storms too hot for keeping,
A sword beneath his mother's heart—yet never
Woman bewept her babe as this is weeping.

A pig with a pasty face, so I had said,
Squealing for cookies, kinned by poor pretense
With a noble house. But the little man quite dead,
I see the forbears' antique lineaments.

The elder men have strode by the box of death
To the wide flag porch, and muttering low send round
The bruit of the day. O friendly waste of breath!
Their hearts are hurt with a deep dynastic wound.

He was pale and little, the foolish neighbors say;
The first-fruits, saith the Preacher, the Lord hath taken;
But this was the old tree's late branch wrenched away,
Grieving the sapless limbs, the shorn and shaken.

First Travels of Max

In that old house of many generations
The best of the Van Vroomans was the youngest.
But even Max, in a chevroned sailor's blouse
And tawny curls far from subdued to the cap,
Had slapped old Katie and removed himself
From games for children; that was because they told
Him never never to set a naughty foot
Into Fool's Forest, where the devil dwelt.

"Become Saint Michael's sword!" said Max to the stick,
And to the stone, "Be a forty-four revolver!"
Then Max was glad that he had armed so wisely
As darker grew the wood, and shrill with silence.
All good fairies were helpless here; at night
Whipped in an inch of their lives; weeping, forbidden
To play with strange scared truant little boys
Who didn't belong there. Snakes were allowed there
And lizards and adders—people of age and evil
That lay on their bellies and whispered—no bird nor rabbit.
There were more rotten trees than there were sound ones.
In that wood timber was degenerate
And rotted almost faster than it grew.
There were no flowers nor apples. Too much age.
The only innocent thing was really Max,
And even he had beat his little sisters.

The black tarn rose up almost in his face.
It was as black and sudden as the pit
The Adversary digs in the bowels of earth;
Bubbles were on it, breath of the black beast
(Formed like a spider, white bag for entrails)
Who took that sort of blackness to inhabit

And dangle after bad men in Fool's Forest.
"Must they be bad?" said casuistical Max.
"Mightn't a good boy who stopped saying his prayers
Be allowed to slip into the spider's fingers?"
Max raised his sword—but what can swords do
Against the Prince of the Dark? Max sheathed his point
And crept around the pool.

There in the middle of the wood was the Red Witch.
Max half expected her. He never imagined
A witch's house that would be red and dirty,
Or a witch's bosom wide and yellow as butter,
Or one that combed so many obscene things
From her black hair into her scarlet lap;
He never believed there would attempt to sing
The one that taught the rats to squeal and Bashan's
Bull to bellow.

"Littlest and last Van Vrooman, do you come too?"
She knew him, it appeared, would know him better,
The scarlet hulk of hell with a fat bosom
Pirouetting at the bottom of the forest.
Certainly Max had come, but he was going;
Unequal contests never being commanded
On young knights only armed in innocence.
"When I am a grown man I will come here
And cut your head off!" That was very well.
And no true heart beating in Christendom
Could have said more, but that for the present would do.

Max went straight home, and nothing chilled him more
Than the company kept him by the witch's laugh
And the witch's song, and the creeping of his flesh.

Max is more firmly domiciliated.
A great house is Van Vrooman, a green slope
South to the sun do the great ones inhabit,

And a few children play on the lawn with the nurse.
Max has returned to his play, and you may find him,
His famous curls unsmoothed, if you will call
Where the Van Vroomans live; the tribe Van Vrooman
Live there at least when any are at home.

Necrological

The friar had said his paternosters duly
And scourged his limbs, and afterwards would have slept;
But with much riddling his head became unruly,
He arose, from the quiet monastery he crept.

Dawn lightened the place where the battle had been won.
The people were dead—it is easy he thought to die—
These dead remained, but the living all were gone,
Gone with the wailing trumps of victory.

The dead men wore no raiment against the air,
Bartholomew's men had spoiled them where they fell;
In defeat the heroes' bodies were whitely bare,
The field was white like meads of asphodel.

Not all were white; some gory and fabulous
Whom the sword had pierced and then the gray wolf eaten;
But the brother reasoned that heroes' flesh was thus;
Flesh fails, and the postured bones lie weather-beaten.

The lords of chivalry lay prone and shattered,
The gentle and the bodyguard of yeomen;
Bartholomew's stroke went home—but little it mattered,
Bartholomew went to be stricken of other foemen.

Beneath the blue ogive of the firmament
Was a dead warrior, clutching whose mighty knees
Was a leman, who with her flame had warmed his tent,
For him enduring all men's pleasantries.

Close by the sable stream that purged the plain
Lay the white stallion and his rider thrown,

The great beast had spilled there his little brain,
And the little groin of the knight was spilled by a stone.

The youth possessed him then of a crooked blade
Deep in the belly of a lugubrious wight;
He fingered it well, and it was cunningly made;
But strange apparatus was it for a Carmelite.

He sat upon a hill and bowed his head
As under a riddle, and in a deep surmise
So still that he likened himself unto those dead
Whom the kites of Heaven solicited with sweet cries.

Captain Carpenter

Captain Carpenter rose up in his prime
Put on his pistols and went riding out
But had got wellnigh nowhere at that time
Till he fell in with ladies in a rout.

It was a pretty lady and all her train
That played with him so sweetly but before
An hour she'd taken a sword with all her main
And twined him of his nose for evermore.

Captain Carpenter mounted up one day
And rode straightway into a stranger rogue
That looked unchristian but be that as may
The Captain did not wait upon prologue.

But drew upon him out of his great heart
The other swung against him with a club
And cracked his two legs at the shinny part
And let him roll and stick like any tub.

Captain Carpenter rode many a time
From male and female took he sundry harms
He met the wife of Satan crying "I'm
The she-wolf bids you shall bear no more arms."

Their strokes and counters whistled in the wind
I wish he had delivered half his blows
But where she should have made off like a hind
The bitch bit off his arms at the elbows.

And Captain Carpenter parted with his ears
To a black devil that used him in this wise

O Jesus ere his threescore and ten years
Another had plucked out his sweet blue eyes.

Captain Carpenter got up on his roan
And sallied from the gate in hell's despite
I heard him asking in the grimmest tone
If any enemy yet there was to fight?

"To any adversary it is fame
If he risk to be wounded by my tongue
Or burnt in two beneath my red heart's flame
Such are the perils he is cast among.

"But if he can he has a pretty choice
From an anatomy with little to lose
Whether he cut my tongue and take my voice
Or whether it be my round red heart he choose."

It was the neatest knave that ever was seen
Stepping in perfume from his lady's bower
Who at this word put in his merry mien
And fell on Captain Carpenter like a tower.

I would not knock old fellows in the dust
But there lay Captain Carpenter on his back
His weapons were the old heart in his bust
And a blade shook between rotten teeth alack.

The rogue in scarlet and grey soon knew his mind
He wished to get his trophy and depart
With gentle apology and touch refined
He pierced him and produced the Captain's heart.

God's mercy rest on Captain Carpenter now
I thought him Sirs an honest gentleman
Citizen husband soldier and scholar enow
Let jangling kites eat of him if they can.

But God's deep curses follow after those
That shore him of his goodly nose and ears
His legs and strong arms at the two elbows
And eyes that had not watered seventy years.

The curse of hell upon the sleek upstart
That got the Captain finally on his back
And took the red red vitals of his heart
And made the kites to whet their beaks clack clack.

Spiel of Three Mountebanks

THE SWARTHY ONE—
Villagers who gather round,
This is Fides, my lean hound.
Bring your bristled village curs
To try his fang and tooth, sweet sirs!
He will rend them, he is savage,
Thinking nothing but to ravage,
Nor with cudgel, fire, rope,
May you control my misanthrope;
He would tear the moon in the sky
And fly at Heaven, could he fly.
And for his ravening without cease
I have had of him no peace;
Only once I bared the knife
To quit my devil of his life,
But listen, how I heard him say,
"Think you I shall die today?
Since your mother cursed and died,
I am keeping at your side,
We are firmly knit together,
Two ends tugging at one tether,
And you shall see when I shall die
That you are mortal even as I."
Bring your stoutest-hearted curs
If you would risk him, gentle sirs.

THE THICK ONE—
Countrymen, here's a noble frame,
Humphrey is my elephant's name.
When my father's back was bent
Under steep impediment,
Humphrey came to my possession,

4 7

With patient strength for all his passion.
Have you a mountain to remove?
It is Humphrey's dearest love.
Pile his burden to the skies,
Loose a pestilence of flies,
Foot him in the quick morass
Where no laden beast can pass,
He will staunch his weariless back
And march unswerving on the track.
Have you seen a back so wide,
So impenetrable hide?
Nor think you by this Humphrey hill
Prince Hamlet bare his fardels ill?
Myself, I like it not for us
To wear beneath an incubus,
I take offence, but in no rage
May I dispose my heritage;
Though in good time the vast and tough
Shall sink and totter fast enough.
So pile your population up,
They are a drop in Humphrey's cup;
Add all your curses to his pack
To make one straw for Humphrey's back.

THE PALE ONE—

If you remark how poor I am,
Come, citizens, behold my lamb!
Have you a lion, ounce, or scourge,
Or any beast of dainty gorge?
Agnus lays his tender youth
Between the very enemy's mouth.
And though he sniff his delicate meat
He may not bruise that flesh nor eat,
He may not rend him limb from limb
If Agnus do but bleat on him.
Fierce was my youth, but like a dream
I saw a temple and a stream,
And where I knelt and washed my sore,

48

This infant lamb stood on the shore,
He mounted with me from the river,
And still he cries, as brave as ever:
"Lay me down by the lion's side
To match my frailty with his pride.
Fain would I welter in my blood
To teach these lions true lionhood."
So daily Agnus would be slain
But daily is denied again,
And still the hungry lions range
While Agnus waits upon a change;
Only the coursing lions die
And in their deserts mortify.
So bring us lion, leopard, bear,
To try of Agnus without fear,
And you less gentle than I am,
Come, be instructed of my Lamb.

Nocturne

Where now has our young Adam
Gone from his sultry Eden,
And where is that Goat-footed
Chasing his willing maiden?
Our man shall cut few capers
In his dark seersucker coat,
With gravest eye subduing
The outrageous tie at his throat;
Wondering if he should carry
His dutiful flesh to the ball,
Or open books that are symbols
And rules and manual.

The intellect bore so hard
Upon the tortured blood,
It dried to a quaint quintessence
The dignities of manhood;
The rivers have passed the bridges
And riding far and free,
Have pitched his boats of passion
Into the sportive sea;
No storm is in this dusk,
But there's a distant flash
That signals brine and foam
And booming floods that thrash.

But still the plum-tree blooms
Despite the rocks at root,
Despite that everyone knows
Its wizened and little fruit;
And the white moon plunges wildly
Like an ubiquitous ghost,

Seeking her own old people
Who are a long time lost;
Till he is almost persuaded
And might yet go to the ball,
If head would concede to heart
A trip to the bacchanal.

Dog

Cock-a-doodle-doo the brass-lined rooster goes,
Brekekekex intones the fat Greek frog,
These fantasies do not worry me as does
The bow-wow-wow of dog.

I had a doggie who used to sit and beg,
A pretty little creature with tears in his eyes
And anomalous hand extended on a leg.
Housebroken was my Huendchen, and so wise.

Booms a big dog's voice like a fireman's bell.
But Fido sits at dusk on Madame's lap
And bored beyond his tongue's poor skill to tell
Rehearses his pink paradigm, To yap.

However. Up the lane the tender bull
Proceeds unto his kine; he yearns for them,
Whose eyes adore him and are beautiful,
Love speeds him, and no treason or mayhem.

But having come to the gateway in the fence,
Listen! again the hateful barking dog,
Like a numerous army rattling the battlements
With shout, though it is but his monologue,
With lion's courage and sting-bee's virulence
Though he is but one dog.

Shrill is the fury of the royal bull,
His knees quiver, and the honeysuckle vine
Expires with anguish as his voice, dreadful,
Cries, "What do you want of my bonded lady kine?"

Now the air trembles to the sorrowing Moo
Of twenty blameless ladies of the mead
Who fear their lord's precarious set-to.
It is the sunset and the heavens bleed.

The hooves of the brave bull slither the claybank
And cut the green tendrils of the vine; the horn
Slices the young birch into splinter and shank
But lunging leaves the bitch's boy untorn.

Across the late sky comes master, Hodge by name,
Upright, two-legged, tall-browed, and self-assured,
In his hand a cudgel, in his blue eye a flame:
"Have I beat my dog so sore and he is not cured?"

Old Hodge stays not his hand, but whips to kennel
The renegade. God's peace betide the souls
Of the pure in heart! But from the box in the fennel
Blaze two red eyes as hot as cooking-coals.

Blackberry Winter

If there be a power of sweetness, let it lie,
For being drunken with steam of Cuban cigars
He takes no pungence from the odor of stars,
And even his music stops on one long sigh.

Still he must sing to his virgin apple tree
Who has not borne him a winey beauty of red;
The silver blooms and bronzy nubs drop dead
But the nonpareil may ripen yet, maybe.

Bestarred is the Daughter of Heaven's house, and cold,
He has seen her often, she sat all night on the hill,
Unseemly the pale youth clambered toward her, till
Untimely the peacock screamed, and he wakened old.

The breath of a girl is music of fall and swell.
Trumpets convolve in the warrior's chambered ear,
But he has listened; none is resounding here,
So much the wars have dwindled since Troy fell.

Armageddon

Antichrist, playing his lissome flute and merry
As was his wont, debouched upon the plain;
Then came a swirl of dust, and Christ drew rein,
Brooding upon his frugal breviary.

Now which shall die, the roundel, rose, and hall,
Or else the tonsured beadsman's monkery?
For Christ and Antichrist arm cap-a-pie,
The prospect charms the soul of the lean jackal.

But Antichrist got down from the Barbary beast
And doffed his plume in courteous prostration;
Christ left his jennet's back in deprecation
And raised him, his own hand about the waist.

Then they must finger chivalry's quaint page,
Of precedence discoursing by the letter.
The oratory of Antichrist was better,
He invested Christ with the elder lineage.

He set Christ on his own Mahomet's back
Where Christ sat fortressed up like Diomede;
The cynical jennet was the other steed,
Obtuse, and most indifferent to attack.

The lordings measured lances and stood still,
And each was loath to let the other's blood;
Originally they were one brotherhood;
There stood the white pavilion on the hill.

To the pavilion went then the hierarchs,
If they might truce their honorable dispute;

Firm was the Christian's chin and he was mute,
And Antichrist ejected scant remarks.

Antichrist tendered a spray of rosemary
To serve his brother for a buttonhole;
Then Christ about his adversary's poll
Wrapped a dry palm that grew on Calvary.

Christ wore a dusty cassock, and the knight
Did him the honors of his tiring-hall,
Whence Christ did not come forth too finical
In his egregious beauty richly dight.

With feasting they concluded every day,
And when the other shaped his phrases thicker
Christ, introducing water in the liquor,
Made wine of more ethereal bouquet.

At wassail Antichrist would pitch the strain
For unison of all the retinue;
Christ beat the time, and hummed a stave or two,
But did not say the words, which were profane.

Perruquiers were privily presented,
Till, knowing his need extreme and his heart pure,
Christ let them dress him his thick chevelure,
And soon his beard was glozed and sweetly scented.

And so the Wolf said Brother to the Lamb,
The True Heir keeping with the poor Impostor,
The rubric and the holy paternoster
Were jangled strangely with the dithyramb.

It could not be. There was a patriarch,
A godly liege of old malignant brood
Who could not fathom the new brotherhood
Between the children of the light and dark.

He sought the ear of Christ on these doings
But in the white pavilion when he stood
And saw them favored and dressed like twins at food,
Profound and mad became his misgivings.

The voices, and their burdens, he must hear,
But equal between the pleasant Princes flew
Theology, art, the old customs and new;
Hoarsely he ran and hissed—in the wrong ear!

He was discomfited, but Christ much more.
Christ sheds unmannerly his devil's pelf,
Takes ashes from the hearth and smears himself,
Calls for his smock and jennet as before.

His trump recalls his own to right opinions,
With scourge they mortify their carnal selves,
With stone they whet the ax-heads on the helves
And seek the Prince Beelzebub and minions.

Christ and his myrmidons, Christ at the head,
Chanted of death and glory and no complaisance;
Antichrist and the armies of malfeasance
Made songs of innocence and no bloodshed.

The immortal Adversary shook his head;
If now they fought too long, why, he would famish;
And if much blood was shed he would be squeamish.
"These Armageddons!" he said; and later bled.

Old Man Playing with Children

A discreet householder exclaims on the grandsire
In warpaint and feathers, with fierce grandsons and axes
Dancing round a backyard fire of boxes:
"Watch grandfather, he'll set the house on fire."

But I will unriddle for you the thought of his mind,
An old one you cannot open with conversation.
What animates the thin legs in risky motion?
Mixes the snow on the head with snow on the wind?

"Grandson, grandsire. We are equally boy and boy.
Do not offer your reclining-chair and slippers
With tedious old women talking in wrappers.
This life is not good but in danger and in joy.

"It is you the elder to these and junior to me
Who are penned as slaves by properties and causes
And never walk from your insupportable houses.
Shamefully, when boys shout, you turn and flee.

"May God forgive me, I know your middling ways,
Having taken care and performed ignominies unreckoned
Between the first brief childhood and brief second,
But I will be more honorable in these days."

Prometheus in Straits

Windy gentlemen wreathing a long verandah,
With tongues busy between illicit potations
Assailing all the acta and/or agenda
Of previous and/or present administrations:
Observe that I'm carefully jotting no memoranda
Lest I seem to identify your wits with your nation's.

But now approaches the radiant band all spinster
Of spirits weaving delirious rhythms of chatter
About old picture galleries and Westminster;
My sensitivity's out of this world, it is utter;
I wish I were a patriarch jungle monster;
The parrots' bonnets, yes; but stop the twitter.

To the colleges then, and the modern masterpieces?
Not now, though I risk the damage of your inference;
Before your explications respect ceases
For centers lost in so absurd circumference;
You have only betrayed them by your exegesis
And provoke me to gestures not of deference.

Though I be Prometheus my mind may have wandered
In bringing my pious offices to this people;
Where all must be teachers, nullity is engendered
And doctrine perishes crying for an ear which is simple;
The prophet is solicited before he has well thundered
And escapes with credit if he do not turn disciple.

At least my function concerns itself with your planet
And due distinctions of faith and fact and fiction;

I will go somewhere by a streamside abounding with granite
And but little human history and dereliction;
To the Man Unknown I will raise an altar upon it
And practise my knees with bruises of genuflection.

Our Two Worthies

All the here and all the there
Ring with the praises of the pair:
Jesus the Paraclete
And Saint Paul the Exegete.

Jesus proclaimed the truth.
Paul's missionary tooth
Shredded it fine, and made a paste,
No particle going to waste,
Kneaded it and caked it
And buttered it and baked it
(And indeed all but digested
While Jesus went to death and rested)
Into a marketable compound
Ready to lay on any wound,
Meet to prescribe to our distress
And feed unto our emptiness.

And this is how the Pure Idea
Became our perfect panacea,
Both external and internal
And supernal and infernal.

When the great captains die,
There is some faithful standing by
To whom the chieftain hands his sword.
Proud Paul received—a Word.

This was the man who, given his cause,
Gave constitution and by-laws,
Distinguished pedagogue
Who invaded the synagogue

6 1

And in a little while
Was proselyting the Gentile.

But what would there have been for Paul
If the Source had finished all?
He blessed the mighty Paraclete
For needing him, to miss defeat,
He couldn't have done anything
But for his Captain spiriting.

He knew that he was competent
For any sort of punishment,
With his irresistible urge
To bare his back unto the scourge,
Teasing his own neck
In prodigious shipwreck;
Hunger and rats and gaol
Were mere detail.

Paul was every inch of him
Valiant as the Seraphim,
And all he went among
Confessed his marvelous tongue,
And Satan fearing the man's spell
Embittered smote the gates of Hell.
So he finished his fight
And he too went from sight.

Then let no cantankerous schism
Corrupt this our catechism
But one and all let us repeat:
Who then is Jesus?
He is our Paraclete.
And Paul, out of Tarsus?
He is our Exegete.

Philomela

Procne, Philomela, and Itylus,
Your names are liquid, your improbable tale
Is recited in the classic numbers of the nightingale.
Ah, but our numbers are not felicitous,
It goes not liquidly for us.

Perched on a Roman ilex, and duly apostrophized,
The nightingale descanted unto Ovid;
She has even appeared to the Teutons, the swilled and gravid;
At Fontainebleau it may be the bird was gallicized;
Never was she baptized.

To England came Philomela with her pain,
Fleeing the hawk her husband; querulous ghost,
She wanders when he sits heavy on his roost,
Utters herself in the original again,
The untranslatable refrain.

Not to these shores she came! this other Thrace,
Environ barbarous to the royal Attic;
How could her delicate dirge run democratic,
Delivered in a cloudless boundless public place
To an inordinate race?

I pernoctated with the Oxford students once,
And in the quadrangles, in the cloisters, on the Cher,
Precociously knocked at antique doors ajar,
Fatuously touched the hems of the hierophants,
Sick of my dissonance.

I went out to Bagley Wood, I climbed the hill;
Even the moon had slanted off in a twinkling,

I heard the sepulchral owl and a few bells tinkling,
There was no more villainous day to unfulfil,
The diuturnity was still.

Out of the darkness where Philomela sat,
Her fairy numbers issued. What then ailed me?
My ears are called capacious but they failed me,
Her classics registered a little flat!
I rose, and venomously spat.

Philomela, Philomela, lover of song,
I am in despair if we may make us worthy,
A bantering breed sophistical and swarthy;
Unto more beautiful, persistently more young,
Thy fabulous provinces belong.

Crocodile

In due season the amphibious crocodile
Rose from the waves and clambered on the bank
And clothed himself, having cleansed his toes which stank
Of bayous of Florida and estuaries of Nile.

And if he had had not water on his brain,
Remember what joys were his. The complete landlubber
In a green mackintosh and overshoes of rubber—
Putting his umbrella up against the rain

For fear of the influenza—sleeking his curls—
Prowling among the petticoats and the teacups—
Visiting the punchbowl to the verge of hiccups—
Breaching his promises and playing with the girls.

At length in grey spats he must cross the ocean.
So this is Paris? Lafayette, we are here.
Bring us sweet wines but none of your French beer!
And he weeps on Notre Dame with proper emotion.

This is Rive Gauche, here's the Hotel Crillon.
Where are the brave poilus? They are slain by his French.
And suddenly he cries, I want to see a trench!
Up in the North eventually he sees one

Which is all green slime and water; whereupon lewd
Nostalgic tremors assail him; with strangled oaths
He flees; he would be kicking off his clothes
And reverting to his pre-Christian mother's nude.

Next on the Grand Tour is Westminster, and Fleet Street.
His Embassy must present him to King George.

Who is the gentleman having teeth so large?
That is Mr. Crocodile, our renowned æsthete.

To know England really one must try the country
And the week-end parties; he is persuaded to straddle
A yellow beast in a red coat on a flat saddle.
Much too gymnastical are the English gentry.

Surely a Scotch and soda with the Balliol men.
But when old Crocodile rises to speak at the Union
He is too miserably conscious of his bunion
And toes too large for the æsthetic regimen.

It is too too possible he has wandered far
From the simple center of his rugged nature.
I wonder, says he, if I am the sort of creature
To live by projects, travel, affaires du coeur?

Crocodile ponders the marrying of a wife
With a ready-made fortune and ready-made family;
The lady is not a poem; she is a homily,
And he hates the rectangular charms of the virtuous life.

Soberly Crocodile sips of the Eucharist.
But as he meditates the obscene complexes
And infinite involutions of the sexes,
Crocodile could be a psychoanalyst.

But who would ever have thought it took such strength
To whittle the tree of being to its points
While the deep-sea urge cries Largo, and all the joints
Tingle with gross desire of lying at length?

Of all the elements mixed in Crocodile
Water is principal; but water flows
By paths of least resistance; and water goes
Down, down, down; which is proper and infantile.

The earth spins from its poles, and is glared on
By the fierce incessant suns, but here is news
For a note in the fine-print column of Thursday Reviews:
Old Robert Crocodile has packed and gone.

His dear friends cannot find him. The ladies write
As usual but their lavender notes are returned
By the U.S. Postmaster and secretively burned.
He has mysteriously got out of sight.

Crocodile hangs his pretty clothes on a limb
And lies with his fathers, and with his mothers too,
And his brothers and sisters as it seems right to do;
The family religion is good enough for him.

Full length he lies and goes as water goes,
He weeps for joy and welters in the flood,
Floating he lies extended nearly a rood,
And quite invisible but for the end of his nose.

Survey of Literature

In all the good Greek of Plato
I lack my roastbeef and potato.

A better man was Aristotle,
Pulling steady on the bottle.

I dip my hat to Chaucer,
Swilling soup from his saucer,

And to Master Shakespeare
Who wrote big on small beer.

The abstemious Wordsworth
Subsisted on a curd's-worth,

But a slick one was Tennyson,
Putting gravy on his venison.

What these men had to eat and drink
Is what we say and what we think.

The influence of Milton
Came wry out of Stilton.

Sing a song for Percy Shelley,
Drowned in pale lemon jelly,

And for precious John Keats,
Dripping blood of pickled beets.

Then there was poor Willie Blake,
He foundered on too sweet cake.

God have mercy on the sinner
Who must write with no dinner,

No gravy and no grub,
No pewter and no pub,

No belly and no bowels,
Only consonants and vowels.

Old Mansion

(*After Henry James*)

As an intruder I trudged with careful innocence
To mask in decency a meddlesome stare,
Passing the old house often on its eminence,
Exhaling my foreign weed on its weighted air.

Here age seemed newly imaged for the historian
After his monstrous châteaux on the Loire,
A beauty not for depicting by old vulgarian
Reiterations that gentle readers abhor.

It was a Southern manor. One hardly imagines
Towers, arcades, or forbidding fortress walls;
But sufficient state though its peacocks now were pigeons;
Where no courts kept, but grave rites and funerals.

Indeed, not distant, possibly not external
To the property, were tombstones, where the catafalque
Had carried their dead; and projected a note too charnel
But for the honeysuckle on its intricate stalk.

Stability was the character of its rectangle
Whose line was seen in part and guessed in part
Through trees. Decay was the tone of old brick and shingle.
Green shutters dragging frightened the watchful heart

To assert: Your mansion, long and richly inhabited,
Its porches and bowers suiting the children of men,
Will not forever be thus, O man, exhibited,
And one had best hurry to enter it if one can.

And at last, with my happier angel's own temerity,
Did I clang their brazen knocker against the door,

To beg their dole of a look, in simple charity,
Or crumbs of wisdom dropping from their great store.

But it came to nothing—and may so gross denial
Which has been deplored with a beating of the breast
Never shorten the tired historian, loyal
To acknowledge defeat and discover a new quest.

The old mistress was ill, and sent my dismissal
By one even more wrappered and lean and dark
Than that warped concierge and imperturbable vassal
Who had bid me begone from her master's Gothic park.

Emphatically, the old house crumbled; the ruins
Would litter, as already the leaves, this petted sward;
And no annalist went in to the lords or the peons;
The antiquary would finger the bits of shard.

But on retreating I saw myself in the token,
How loving from my dying weed the feather curled
On the languid air; and I went with courage shaken
To dip, alas, into some unseemlier world.

On the Road to Wockensutter

(*a Western*)

"Sahara doth not keep her livid hell
Wholly unto herself," said Herodote;
"Sirocco scourgeth even the greenlands well,
The pulver of his brimstone scratched my throat."

Brady had little Latin and less Greek,
Not his to verify the obscure citation,
But Brady knew no waterfall nor creek
Nor Arctic tremor stayed his oxidation.

By sixty fiery miles they call a trail
Red Rock communicates with Wockensutter,
And Brady, who had started on a rail,
Pursued his march diminishing like butter.

For Brady had deployed the manifold
Beneath the holy principle of Venus,
Till desert ladies named him greasy and old,
And the empanelled peers pronounced it heinous.

"She was my Star, and now forbidden me?"
Cried Brady, his faith quivering with outrage;
Then heard and saw the yellow pert pewee
Who flashed across the acrid sea of sage.

Noon of the second day made his ascension,
The Brady marched emblistered for the goal,
And to the pewee made offensive mention
Of words that scored the tablets of her soul.

"A simple shotgun with a choke were best,"
Says Brady, looking for a spot to sit;

But now eluded of Burd Helen's breast
He adds, "Could any human engine hit.

"Venus you are, and we are long acquainted,
I know your signs in any shape and weather,
And even if mortal dared, I have not wanted
To harm a little bird that's false of feather.

"And look, Transfigured! How rightly you betray
To a right man your woman's beauty and bounty.
But I have given my oath. 'Tis sad to say,
My Wockensutter lies in Christian County.

"You smile? I melt—by virtue of my hot rock.
Hadn't we best say farewell altogether?
I'm balancing my years against my luck
Hoping I'll never wonder which or whether."

Morning

Jane awoke Ralph so gently on one morning
That first, before the true householder Learning
Came back to tenant in the haunted head,
He lay upon his back and let his stare
Penetrate dazedly into the blue air
That swam all round his bed,
And in the blessed silence nothing was said.

Then his eyes travelled through the window
And lit, enchantedly, on such a meadow
Of wings and light and clover,
He would propose to Jane then to go walking
Through the green waves, and to be singing not talking;
Such imps were pranking over
Him helpless lying in bed beneath a cover.

Suddenly he remembered about himself,
His manliness returned entire to Ralph;
The dutiful mills of the brain
Began to whir with their smooth-grinding wheels
And the sly visitors wriggled off like eels;
He rose and was himself again.
Simply another morning, and simply Jane.

Jack's Letter

Do not imagine that Jack and Rose apart
Can thrive much, for they cannot lie together
Under the same roof or the same weather.
These are the moons of absence grieving the heart.

If I knew any gods upon the hill,
I'd ask the kindest: Wet your lips and bless
The little ones that die of separateness,
Absent and impotent and unspoken still.

But Jack has wits which he would put to use;
He would convey to Rose his pent-up love
And duly receive acknowledgement thereof.
A letter is his proper and pure excuse.

Too cold and dry he finds the paper sheet,
And atrabilious and sour is ink;
He'd set his matter forth but stops to think
His passion must in transit lose its heat;

So plants on four sides of the folio
Himself in bulbs of cunning charactery,
But Rose must guess the cipher, seeing she
Must water him with tears if he would grow.

The glade is not so green now, Jack says there;
The fish have all gone down the dwindling stream;
The birds have scattered and become a dream;
Himself works with his flowers and goes nowhere.

Here then lies Jack beneath a penny seal.
The dainty lady of the superscription

If she have very delicate perception
With eyes may see and with nice fingers feel.

The post is gone, and the event will tell.
If only she will hug it to her bosom
Her parcel soon will thicken to a blossom
Which will be soft to hold and sweet to smell.

Persistent Explorer

The noise of water teased his literal ear
Which heard the distant drumming, and so scored:
"Water is falling—it fell—therefore it roared.
Yet something else is there: is it cheer or fear?"

He strode much faster, till on the dizzy brink
His eye confirmed with vision what he'd heard:
"A simple physical water." Again he demurred:
"More than a roaring flashing water, I think."

But listen as he might, look fast or slow,
It was common water, millions of tons of it
Gouging its gorge deeper, and every bit
Was water, the insipid chemical H_2O.

Its thunder smote him somewhat as the loud
Words of the god that rang around a man
Walking by the Mediterranean.
Its cloud of froth was whiter than the cloud

That clothed the goddess sliding down the air
Unto a mountain shepherd, white as she
That issued from the smoke refulgently.
The cloud was, but the goddess was not there.

Deafening was the sound, but never a voice
That talked with him; spacious the spectacle
But it spelled nothing; there was not any spell
Whether to bid him cower or rejoice.

What would he have it spell? He scarcely knew;
Only that water and nothing but water filled

His eyes and ears; only water that spilled;
And if the smoke and rattle of water drew

From the deep thickets of his mind the train,
The fierce fauns and the timid tenants there
That burst their bonds and rushed upon the air,
Why, he must turn and beat them down again.

So be it. And no unreasonable outcry
The pilgrim made; only a rueful grin
Spread over his lips until he drew them in;
He would not sit upon a rock and die.

Many are the ways of dying; witness, if he
Commit himself to the water, and descend
Wrapped in the water, turn water at the end,
Part of a water rolling to the sea.

But there were many ways of living, too,
And let his enemies gibe, but let them say
That he would throw this continent away
And seek another country—as he would do.

Puncture

Darkness was bad as weariness, till Grimes said,
"We've got to have a fire." But in that case
The match must sputter and the flame glare red
On nothing beautiful, and set no seal of grace
On any dead man's face.

And when the flames roared, when the sparks dartled
And quenched in the black sea that closed us round,
I looked at Grimes my dear comrade and startled
His look, blue-bright—and under it a wound
Which bled upon the ground.

"They got you? I have only lost a hat,
I would have sold the affair for three thin dimes,
But they have stuck your side. It must be looked at
And mended." "No, it's an old puncture," said Grimes,
"Which takes to bleeding sometimes."

"Why, Grimes, I never knew your mortal blood
Had wasted for my sake in scarlet streams,
And no word said. A curse on my manhood
If I knew anything! This is my luck which seems
Worse than my evillest dreams."

But when I would have comforted his white flesh
With ointment and flowing water, he said then,
"Get away. Go work on the corpses, if you wish,
Prop their heads up again, wrap their bones in,
They were good pious men."

I, not to weep then, like a desperado
Kicked on the carcasses of our enemies

To heave them into the darkness; but my bravado
Quailed in the scorn of Grimes; for even these
Were fit for better courtesies.

Blue blazed the eyes of Grimes in the old manner—
The flames of eyes which jewel the head of youth
Were strange in the leathery phiz of the old campaigner—
Smoke and a dry word crackled from his mouth
Which a cold wind ferried south.

Man without Sense of Direction

Tell this to ladies: how a hero man
Assail a thick and scandalous giant
Who casts true shadow in the sun,
And die, but play no truant.

This is more horrible: that the darling egg
Of the chosen people hatch a creature
Of noblest mind and powerful leg
Who cannot fathom nor perform his nature.

The larks' tongues are never stilled
Where the pale spread straw of sunlight lies;
Then what invidious gods have willed
Him to be seized so otherwise?

Birds of the field and beasts of the stable
Are swollen with rapture and make uncouth
Demonstration of joy, which is a babble
Offending the ear of the fervorless youth.

Love—is it the cause? the proud shamed spirit?
Love has slain some whom it possessed,
But his was requited beyond his merit
And won him in bridal the loveliest.

Yet scarcely he issues from the warm chamber,
Flushed with her passion, when cold as dead
Once more he walks where waves past number
Of sorrow buffet his curse-hung head.

Whether by street, or in field full of honey,
Attended by clouds of the creatures of air

Or shouldering the city's companioning many,
His doom is on him; and how can he care

For the shapes that would fiddle upon his senses,
Wings and faces and mists that move,
Words, sunlight, the blue air which rinses
The pure pale head which he must love?

And he writhes like an antique man of bronze
That is beaten by furies visible,
Yet he is punished not knowing his sins
And for his innocence walks in hell.

He flails his arms, he moves his lips:
"Rage have I none, cause, time, nor country—
Yet I have traveled land and ships
And knelt my seasons in the chantry."

So he stands muttering; and rushes
Back to the tender thing in his charge
With clamoring tongue and taste of ashes
And a small passion to feign large.

But let his cold lips be her omen,
She shall not kiss that harried one
To peace, as men are served by women
Who comfort them in darkness and in sun.

Antique Harvesters

(SCENE: *Of the Mississippi the bank sinister,*
and of the Ohio the bank sinister.)

Tawny are the leaves turned but they still hold,
And it is harvest; what shall this land produce?
A meager hill of kernels, a runnel of juice;
Declension looks from our land, it is old.
Therefore let us assemble, dry, grey, spare,
And mild as yellow air.

"I hear the croak of a raven's funeral wing."
The young men would be joying in the song
Of passionate birds; their memories are not long.
What is it thus rehearsed in sable? "Nothing."
Trust not but the old endure, and shall be older
Than the scornful beholder.

We pluck the spindling ears and gather the corn.
One spot has special yield? "On this spot stood
Heroes and drenched it with their only blood."
And talk meets talk, as echoes from the horn
Of the hunter—echoes are the old men's arts,
Ample are the chambers of their hearts.

Here come the hunters, keepers of a rite;
The horn, the hounds, the lank mares coursing by
Straddled with archetypes of chivalry;
And the fox, lovely ritualist, in flight
Offering his unearthly ghost to quarry;
And the fields, themselves to harry.

Resume, harvesters. The treasure is full bronze
Which you will garner for the Lady, and the moon
Could tinge it no yellower than does this noon;
But grey will quench it shortly—the field, men, stones.
Pluck fast, dreamers; prove as you amble slowly
Not less than men, not wholly.

Bare the arm, dainty youths, bend the knees
Under bronze burdens. And by an autumn tone
As by a grey, as by a green, you will have known
Your famous Lady's image; for so have these;
And if one say that easily will your hands
More prosper in other lands,

Angry as wasp-music be your cry then:
"Forsake the Proud Lady, of the heart of fire,
The look of snow, to the praise of a dwindled choir,
Song of degenerate specters that were men?
The sons of the fathers shall keep her, worthy of
What these have done in love."

True, it is said of our Lady, she ageth.
But see, if you peep shrewdly, she hath not stooped;
Take no thought of her servitors that have drooped,
For we are nothing; and if one talk of death—
Why, the ribs of the earth subsist frail as a breath
If but God wearieth.

The Equilibrists

Full of her long white arms and milky skin
He had a thousand times remembered sin.
Alone in the press of people traveled he,
Minding her jacinth, and myrrh, and ivory.

Mouth he remembered: the quaint orifice
From which came heat that flamed upon the kiss,
Till cold words came down spiral from the head,
Grey doves from the officious tower illsped.

Body: it was a white field ready for love,
On her body's field, with the gaunt tower above,
The lilies grew, beseeching him to take,
If he would pluck and wear them, bruise and break.

Eyes talking: Never mind the cruel words,
Embrace my flowers, but not embrace the swords.
But what they said, the doves came straightway flying
And unsaid: Honor, Honor, they came crying.

Importunate her doves. Too pure, too wise,
Clambering on his shoulder, saying, Arise,
Leave me now, and never let us meet,
Eternal distance now command thy feet.

Predicament indeed, which thus discovers
Honor among thieves, Honor between lovers.
O such a little word is Honor, they feel!
But the grey word is between them cold as steel.

At length I saw these lovers fully were come
Into their torture of equilibrium;

Dreadfully had forsworn each other, and yet
They were bound each to each, and they did not forget.

And rigid as two painful stars, and twirled
About the clustered night their prison world,
They burned with fierce love always to come near,
But Honor beat them back and kept them clear.

Ah, the strict lovers, they are ruined now!
I cried in anger. But with puddled brow
Devising for those gibbeted and brave
Came I descanting: Man, what would you have?

For spin your period out, and draw your breath,
A kinder sæculum begins with Death.
Would you ascend to Heaven and bodiless dwell?
Or take your bodies honorless to Hell?

In Heaven you have heard no marriage is,
No white flesh tinder to your lecheries,
Your male and female tissue sweetly shaped
Sublimed away, and furious blood escaped.

Great lovers lie in Hell, the stubborn ones
Infatuate of the flesh upon the bones;
Stuprate, they rend each other when they kiss,
The pieces kiss again, no end to this.

But still I watched them spinning, orbited nice.
Their flames were not more radiant than their ice.
I dug in the quiet earth and wrought the tomb
And made these lines to memorize their doom: —

EPITAPH

Equilibrists lie here; stranger, tread light;
Close, but untouching in each other's sight;
Mouldered the lips and ashy the tall skull.
Let them lie perilous and beautiful.

To the Scholars of Harvard

Phi Beta Kappa Poem June 23, 1939

When Sarah Pierrepont let her spirit rage
Her love and scorn refused the bauble earth
(Which took bloom even here, under the Bear)
And groped for the Essence, sitting in himself,
Subtle, I think, for a girl's unseasoned rage.

The late and sudden extravagance of soul
By which they all were swollen exalted her
At seventeen years to Edwards' canopy,
A match pleasing to any Heaven, had not
Her twelve mortal labors harassed her soul.

Thrifty and too proud were the sea-borne fathers
Who fetched the Pure Idea in a bound box
And put him into a steeple to have his court
Shabby with an unkingly establishment
And Sabbath levees for the minion fathers.

The majesty of Heaven has a great house,
And even if the Indian kingdom or the fox
Ran barking mad in a wide forest place,
They had his threshold, and you had the dream
Of preference in him by a steepled house.

If once the entail should fall on raffish sons,
Knife-wit scholar and merchant sharp of thumb,
With positive steel they'd pry into the steeple,
And blinking through the cracked ribs at the void
A judgment laughter would rake the cynic sons.

Yet like prevailing wind New England's honor
Carried, and teased small Southern boys at school

Whose heads the temperate birds fleeing your winter
Construed for, but the stiff heroes abashed
With their frozen fingers and unearthly honor.

Scared by the holy megrims of those Pilgrims,
We thought the unhumbled and outcast and cold
Were the rich Heirs traveling incognito,
Bred too fine for the country's sweet produce
And but affecting that dog's life of pilgrims.

There must have been debate of soul and body,
The soul storming incontinent with shrew's tongue
Against what natural brilliance body had loved,
Even the green phases though deciduous
Of Earth's zodiac homage to the body.

Missing stanza here: original had one

Perfect the witch was, foundering in water,
The blasphemer that spraddled in the stocks,
The woman branded with her sin, the whales
Of ocean taken with a psalmer's sword,
The British tea infusing the Bay's water.

But they reared heads into the always clouds
And stooped to the event of war or bread,
The secular perforces and short speech
Being surly labors done with the left hand,
The main strength giddying with transcendent clouds.

The tangent Heavens teased the fathers' strength,
And how the young sons know it, and study now
To make fresh conquest of the conquered earth,
But they're too strong for that, you've seen them whip
The laggard will to deeds of lunatic strength.

To incline the powerful living unto peace
With Heaven is easier now, with earth is hard,
Yet a rare metaphysic makes them one,

A gentle Majesty, whose myrtle and rain
Enforce the fathers' gravestones unto peace.

I saw the youngling bachelors of Harvard
Lit like torches, and scrambling to disperse
Like aimless firebrands pitiful to slake,
And if there's passion enough for half their flame,
Your wisdom has been valiant, sages of Harvard.

What Ducks Require

Ducks require no ship and sail
Bellied on the foamy skies,
Who scud north. Male and female
Make a slight nest to arise
Where they overtake the spring,
Which clogs with muddy going.

The zone unready. But the pond,
Eye of a bleak Cyclops visage, catches
Such glints of hyacinth and bland
As bloom in aquarelles of ditches
On a cold spring ground, a freak,
A weathering chance even in the wrack.

The half-householders for estate
Beam their floor with ribs of grass,
Disdain your mortises and slate
And Lar who invalided lies,
The marsh quakes dangerous, the port
Where wet and dry precisely start.

Furled, then, the quadrate wing
From the lewd eye and fowler's gun
Till in that wet sequestering,
Webtoed, the progeny is done,
Cold-hatched, the infant prodigy tries
To preen his feathers for the skies.

Prodigious in his wide degrees
Who where the winds and waters blow
On raveling banks of fissured seas
In reeds nestles, or will rise and go
Where Capicornus dips his hooves
In the blue chasm of no wharves.

Painted Head

By dark severance the apparition head
Smiles from the air a capital on no
Column or a Platonic perhaps head
On a canvas sky depending from nothing;

Stirs up an old illusion of grandeur
By tickling the instinct of heads to be
Absolute and to try decapitation
And to play truant from the body bush;

But too happy and beautiful for those sorts
Of head (homekeeping heads are happiest)
Discovers maybe thirty unwidowed years
Of not dishonoring the faithful stem;

Is nameless and has authored for the evil
Historian headhunters neither book
Nor state and is therefore distinct from tart
Heads with crowns and guilty gallery heads;

Wherefore the extravagant device of art
Unhousing by abstraction this once head
Was capital irony by a loving hand
That knew the no treason of a head like this;

Makes repentance in an unlovely head
For having vinegarly traduced the flesh
Till, the hurt flesh recusing, the hard egg
Is shrunken to its own deathlike surface;

And an image thus. The body bears the head
(So hardly one they terribly are two)

Feeds and obeys and unto please what end?
Not to the glory of tyrant head but to

The estate of body. Beauty is of body.
The flesh contouring shallowly on a head
Is a rock-garden needing body's love
And best bodiness to colorify

The big blue birds sitting and sea-shell flats
And caves, and on the iron acropolis
To spread the hyacinthine hair and rear
The olive garden for the nightingales.

Two Gentlemen in Bonds

(in twelve sonnets)

I   Pink and Pale

Paul, pinked with dozing, stood from the couch wherein
Digestion was assisted after lunch—
Roast chines and gravies, pudding, swigs of punch,
His manhood being strong and it no sin
To feed—then stretched and tucked his loose ends in
And singing till he had sung himself outside
He went to banter Abbott, or to ride.
Poor company Abbott kept his next of kin.

For everything that Paul was, Abbott was not;
His legs were two long straws, his face was chalk,
He would not ride nor run nor drowse, but walk
The wood in thought more passionate than another's;
You wouldn't believe that two such men were brothers;
Yet it was credited, the same sire begot.

II   Thinking, Drinking

A young girl cousined them, whose character was
A wise bright head, and grey eyes beautifuller
To Paul than his brave manhood seemed to her,
Though he was Greek enough for Phidias,
And she could ride. But about this Michaelmas
She wouldn't go in her green riding habit
To canter with him and hollo to every rabbit
That bounced across to thicket or to grass.

Too much she listened to Abbott's music of words:
"O the wild flood! How noble is man thinking!
But we, my cousin, are filled with eating and drinking.
Should we not read philosophy?" But Paul said,
"Edith, my brother's a fool and out of his head,"
And saw her thoughts fly over him like birds.

III   Epithalamion of a Peach

She was round, full, ripe, a maid immaculate,
Saving her cheeks. Now Paul the hot bridegroom
Acclaims his treasure, his hand has led her home;
Nor did he pull her gently through the gate
As would a lover more dainty and delicate:
The two-and-thirty cut-throats doing his will
Tore off her robes and stripped her down until
He looked upon her bare. Then turned and ate.

Shame on him, juice is drooling from his tongue
Where he has absorbed the admirable peach
Who nested high but not beyond his reach!
It was unloverly work, and brought the wry
To squeamish Abbott's face; not noted by
The oblivious gelding stamping in his dung.

IV   Bad News

It happening in that country that the King
Came now that way victorious in battle
Where he had slain some folk and taken their cattle,
His Chamberlain told Sir Paul a proper thing
For doing: Make ready with feast and furnishing
To lodge the King three days; it would be good
If the King favored his bed and savored his food,
For service improved a man in the sight of his King.

Now purple and linen, or poultry and beef and swine,
He loved not for themselves, but must accept
For his belly's sake, for his body and bed well-kept;
It would impoverish his country house
If the Court descended for a week's carouse.
No more he napped in innocence after wine.

V   *L'etat c'est moi*

Abbott previsioning the pestilent swarm
Of royal locusts: "Expect now, Brother Paul,
A trifling inconvenience; that will be all.
These levies and tributes keep you out of harm,
The thieves the King has slain cause no alarm,
But you have to pay a price for this relief:
Strong Kingdoms always manage to get their beef,
Le Roi lui-même, by grace of *ces gendarmes.*

"It doesn't matter if your King's a fraud,
A gross pig's-bladder prickable as any,
A man whose nose runs probably more than many,
Whose beard shines with its gravy; he is the King,
The State; you are his man, his littlest thing—
Or would you go in hiding and be outlawed?"

VI   Misanthrope

"But I am not of the King's table; nor his stable.
Once we were sovereigns, but there's been interchange.
In the mother-house I dwelt severe and strange
Till they ripped me out by the heels and cut the cable,
A Form whose fixity always turns to fable
By the force of things; am enamored yet of that womb
Which yields no analogue but one, the tomb,
Where Kings may lie and hear their Kingdoms babble.

"My compliments to your King. Say I'm not in.
I'll move to the Northern tower; your misanthrope,
Too firm to be wheedled by fat King or lean Pope,
And all the papal prayers and all King's power
Shall not convey me from my absolute tower.
But you have sensitive skin, so save your skin."

VII   Kingdom Come

To an honest knight if the lucky break befall
That his King visit him, lord of his life and breath
Whose ministers post and cry, "Thus saith, Thus saith,"
His paths prepared by a Chamberlain master of all
Husbandry whispering, "Spare no expense, Sir Paul,"
Noised in the East with horn and hoof and drum,
But weathering West till his plumy host are come
And stand in the gate to hail the loving thrall:

Why, the young heart bursts for shame if such a King,
Helped from his horse, his foxface peaked with travel,
His bowels infirm, his water stopped with gravel,
Must to bed, with a pair of leeches by bedside
And Bishop saying prayers against his pride.
He'll have no stomach for speech of welcoming.

VIII   In Bed Not Dead

"We never dreamed he'd be so bad," said thrall,
And Edith tossed her bright cloud, "Abbott was right,
I cannot endure this creature in my sight."
But they got him in bed and he made no fuss at all,
One day they nursed him, then he put on his shawl
And made them fashion a throne of cushions and things
Where he held court in the strictest manner of Kings,
Whose minions bowed till they almost got their fall.

The fishy hue of the King's eye was not fast,
It veered to a negative green or a yellow smile,
But brain behind was busy in whichever style;
Now the inconstant orb perused Sir Paul
And his pretty calves; he would do for a Seneschal
If aught was above the shoulders; those were vast.

IX   Primer for Statesmen

The King, to a backward scholar of common laws
Politico-biological: "Little brown birds
Seem bent on pleasing us with songs without words
But actually dwell forever upon their craws;
The fiercer beasts work ravin to glut their maws;
The serpent travels in fact upon his belly,
A hardy soul, but according to Machiavelli
This creature has no ear for public applause.

"He never could found a State. But a King can,
By policies wholly according with appetite,
Teaching his subjects the law of Divine Right,
Then with a show of honor despoiling them.
He must tickle with love, and rule by stratagem.
Now give me heed, Sir Paul, and play the man."

X *Fait Accompli*

He summons Edith, which is Paul's own desire.
He finds her very fair, but the face is flushed
And the grey films averted. That storm is hushed
In which she had cried like prophetess on fire
(While the maid smoothed her tangles and attire)
Upon the impossible Kings who broke your peace
And ruled you body and soul beyond release.
He smiles on the timid doe now come to his lair.

He's taken Edith's little left hand, to lay
On Paul's overpowering right. There's no recourse
Except in Paul's recital: "For better, for worse."
On whom is she smiling? "I wish you many joys,
My Kingdom will be better by many boys
If Heaven reward your union, which I pray."

XI   Rain

"Rain is a long susurrance; makes no loud
Clamor, yet mutes the terrible bugles; no night
Yet darkens the insupportable sunlight
And flame-borrowing bush and feather; a cloud
And cool upon your heads, poor wrinkle-browed
Percipiences! Not true Styx, yet a river
Washing the wounded senses of their fever;
A barrier wall let down; or a makeshift shroud.

"Yes, think of the happy dead who fall in the valleys
Of gentle rivers—eyeballs opening wide
To the comfort of that unlit undusty tide—
Ears flowering green and huge beyond the bawling
Of air—and a brief sweet season of tumbling, crawling,
On legs and arms among the waterlilies."

XII   Injured Sire

"Now I remember life; and out of me
Lawfully leaping, the twin seed of my loins,
Brethren, whom no split fatherhood disjoins.
But in the woman-house how hatefully
They trod upon each other! till now I see
My manhood halved and squandered, one head, one heart,
Each partial son despising the other's part.
But so it is; so all their lives 'twill be.

"Yet would it be precarious, wanting to weep
From eyes unfastened, or to shudder with brittle joints.
I am a spectre, even if at some sore points
A father in ill repute with his own issue.
O Lord defend my poor old fragile tissue!
But I'll not risk it. I will turn and sleep."

Sixteen Poems in Eight Pairings

with original and final versions studied comparatively

Preface

Here follows, completing the text of this final edition of *Selected Poems*, a set of pairings or couplings of poems which are closely related. The first poem of each pairing is designated *A*, and reports a vision or a meditation which will just manage as a prompter to the *B* poem, its superior. Let *A* stand for Average, for the sort of poem which is good enough to look for publication. And let *B* stand for Better; I must not say for Best. My purpose is didactic, and even euphuistic: to see how a deficient poem may be whipped into something more satisfactory—if only it has sufficient "makings." As the proverb goes, the poet not only must be "born" with the heritage of an individual talent, but also must be "made" by his own best labor of will and imagination.

I sometimes find myself wishing that the idiom for the two stages of the poem might be "born and bred"; a usage that seems to call for the more admirable actions and sentiments of mankind, therefore steeped in morals and manners. But always on second thought it occurs to me that we require also a poetry of many humors, of satire, and even of naked evil. That kind of poetry would be permissive, and instructive as to one of the built-in halves of our personalities. And I do not recall many ages whose poets at large have dwelt more insistently upon evil than have those of our own generation. They display on purpose the dark and animal side of our divided selves; but probably, with or without knowing it, they mean to remind themselves and the rest of us of the parity of the two sides. This is the principle of old Heraclitus himself, now renewed with great rigor;

and I for one have not resisted it. I must have observed several times in print that the man who limits himself, aspiring to pure goodness or saintliness, seems to us very far from possessing that entire vitality which Providence has meant for him. He has not elected the whole joy of life.

The date and publisher of each *A* poem will be recorded as we come to it. But it needs to be stated positively that the date of all the *B* poems is Now; they are final versions that have been arrived at in this year of 1968. Furthermore, I have revised, and promoted to the text of *Selected Poems*, a dozen or so poems which existed in my three single volumes: in *Poems About God*, Henry Holt, 1919; in *Chills and Fever*, Alfred A. Knopf, 1924; and in *Two Gentlemen in Bonds*, Alfred A. Knopf, 1927.

Overturcs

A

My dear and I, we disagreed
When we had been much time together.
For when will lovers learn to sail
If sailing always in good weather?

She said a hateful little word
Between the pages of the book.
I bubbled with a noble rage,
I bruised her with a dreadful look,

And thanked her kindly for the word
Of such a little silly thing;
Indeed I loved my poet then
Beyond my dear, or anything.

And she, the proud girl, swept away,
How swift and scornfully she went!
And I the frightened lover stayed
And have not had one hour's content

Until today; until I knew
That I was loved again, again;
Then hazard how this thing befell,
Brother of women and of men.

"Perhaps a gallant gentleman
Accomplished it, who saw you bleed;
Perhaps she wrote upon the book
A riddling thing that you could read;

"Perhaps she crept to you and cried,
And took upon her all the blame."

O no, do proud girls cry for shame?
"Perhaps she whispered you your name."

O no, she walked alone, and I
Was walking in the rainy wood,
And saw her drooping by the tree,
And saw my work of widowhood.

COMMENT

The poem was published in *Poems About God*, Henry Holt, 1919. I had promised myself never to republish any of its contents, by reason of the general poverty of its style, and its blatant and inconsistent theologizing. But I recently gave it a final reading, and was impressed by the charming moment when the speaker stops his narrative and calls upon his friend to "hazard how this thing befell." The friend complies ingeniously but without success, and the speaker tells the true story in short order and memorable phrases.

But the poem is deformed by many stylistic and technical errors. In the third stanza I rimed "thing" with "anything," which is repetitive; in the two final lines doubled the phrase, "And saw . . . And saw"; and in general made too many lines beginning with "And." In the fifth stanza I address the friend as "Brother of women and of men." That would mean, ordinarily, that he is a member of a large family having at least three brothers and two sisters; who might, if they chose, quarrel incessantly with each other without disputing my phrase. It would be more to the point if the friend was "Brother to women and to men"; meaning that he "brothered" all women and men in trouble to whom he might bring comfort and relief. In the two stanzas of the friend's response I was wholly correct in punctuating them with five quotation marks, in the right places. But I wanted to be sure, and therefore, for good measure, distinguished the friend's lines by italicizing them; a disconcerting superfluity. The final line has the truant bride "drooping by the tree." But what tree was it, in all that "rainy wood?" We probably are correct in assuming that it was the "trysting-tree," or whatever tree might be the one beneath which the bride had been courted and won. Her drooping there would be the symbol of remorse, and would lead to a reconciliation and a happy ending.

Two Gentlemen Scholars

(a pastoral)

B

The scene is a private study,
in late evening.

FRIEND
Tell the whole history which I crave
And I'll go, secret as the grave.

HUSBAND
Neighbors, in woodland half-begirt
With ribbon of silver, mine and hers,
We walked like knowing foresters
Till I spoke rime, and she looked hurt.

Soon she was bride beneath my roof.
We walked like pilgrims by the stream,
The whiles I sang she took to dream,
My younger songster, still aloof.

Now we have spent sweet moon together,
But Lord! even we must disagree.
Shall not bold mariner rule the sea
Though sailing in the worst of weather?

On one page of my poet's book
She wrote a little hateful screed.
I could have shook her like a reed
But I did bleed her with a look,

And thanked her for her kind opinion,
That from a girl who wore my ring!
I said that some day she might sing
But John Donne kept his sure dominion.

She flung my ring upon the floor,
Exchanging scorns, and went her way.

But I have tarried day by day
A cast-off lover by my own door,

Until this morning early; when
A midnight thought had augured well.
Now will you hazard what befell,
Brother to women and to men?

FRIEND
Perhaps a virtuous gentleman
Accomplished it, who saw her bleed?
Or did she send if you would read
A riddling verse if you could scan?

Well then, she crept to you and cried
And took upon her all the blame.

HUSBAND
O no, do proud girls cry for shame?

FRIEND
The rainstorm sent her to your side.

HUSBAND
Never. My kingly moment came.
I'd find her by the siren stream
And careless how she'd fight or fume
I'd clutch her tight and take her home.

FRIEND
And call a truce?

HUSBAND
           Just say that I
Meandering in the rainy wood
Beheld her drooping by the flood.
She's resting now. I ask you why

Kingdom may not go twice awry?
I have repaired one widowhood.

I peer into your fearful mind.
Be you a king, and do you anoint
Her as a queen, two sovereigns joint.
O, never again be you unkind,
Nor even tutorial. Let her find
Her own words, up to the breaking point.

Her voice is modern, and we know those
Young bards who listen to the birds
And sing with insufficient words.
Yes! Fate, uneasy, may propose
A second reckoning with her woes
Whose lute is tuned to such discords.

HUSBAND
You've fed my fears. She'll fly again
To the hurtling wave, and before I come
She's jumped! and how shall I get her home?
May the Lord deliver us from that pain.

FRIEND
I love you well, and I'll not tell.

(*Exit*)

COMMENT

The *A* poem used the ballad stanza, the rime pattern being *xaxa*, the measure four beats for each line. Even if the lines were rimed in the pattern *abab* it would remain a ballad, though a more sophisticated one, of which the two speakers are entirely capable. But *B* goes farther: it rimes every line, but the pattern is *abba*. The poem is no longer a ballad; the second line does not rime with the fourth. Often there is some heavy punctuation following one or both of the *b* lines, but that does not keep the argument from being consecutive. The two scholars must know that *In Memoriam*, Tennyson's most important poem, in 131 sections, adapts even these middle rimes to the argument of the stanza with no trouble at all; they become more special and brilliant than they might have been otherwise. And as for the music of the present speakers, in the same pattern, they like the *bb* lines as if they were a special bonus, and did not merely carry a meaning that was vital to their outer envelope. But perhaps it is their special pleasure to wait, with more and more tension, for the moment when the final *a* utters its perfect and climactic concord with the first *a*. The operation has been total and successful.

Now as to the duologue between friend and husband. Both are gentlemen scholars; and poets of some sort, employing the "traditional" or Renaissance style of verse; and their speech is pastoral because they have chosen to live in the country, and the country has much to do with their interests. The errant bride has been found and returned by the husband, and is sleeping upstairs while the gentlemen talk below. The husband has not cared to publish his woes, and the friend knows that it is very late in the evening of a very difficult day; he will not be staying very late, and in no event will he tell what the husband has said.

The *B* version keeps as much as it dares of the language of *A*. It is twice as long; that is because there must be two preliminary stanzas detailing the courtship and marriage of the pair very briefly; and after re-doing the eight stanzas of *A*, the text of *B* must go on past the reconciliation and foreshadow darkly a possible second truancy on the part of the bride which would almost certainly be fatal.

The most grievous blunder of the *A* story is in its last stanza, where the bride is found "drooping by the tree." For the tree does not suggest a mortal danger. The bride-poet must have a body of water to droop by, and to enter, if she has found no success with her art. There is melody in the phrases of *A*'s last stanza, with its "walking in the rainy wood," and "drooping by the tree," and finally: "And saw my work of widowhood." But the *B* version is better in style and more appropriate: "Meandering in the rainy wood/ Beheld her drooping by the flood"; plus the final, "I have repaired one widowhood." The first two lines of *B* introduce the water; husband and bride had been "Neighbors, in woodland half-begirt/ With ribbon of silver." We find in the total *B* version five different and significant phrases for the water: The "ribbon of silver," speaking metaphorically of a flowing water which bends sharply halfway round the woodland; "the stream," the exact word, in stanza two, along with the information that, given their honeymoon, husband and bride had "walked like pilgrims by the stream," because it was there that he had won her; then, "the siren stream," in *B*'s stanza nine. The classical adjective is very important, as if the stream were inviting her to enter into its fluid and silvery element. It may be that she has always loved the stream, with something like a psychic fixation. At any rate she is perfectly fearless, and ready to die as becomingly as possible if her poetic progress fails. In the same stanza the husband indicates without too close detail that he has brought her home by main force. But the *B* version is not finished till the husband has asked the friend if "Kingdom may not go twice awry?" and the friend has replied that it might easily happen. This time the husband names the stream a fourth time, to say that she will "fly again/ To the hurtling wave," and make her mortal jump before he can come to her. But she is not yet doomed by Fate to that extremity. The action is indeterminate; and we are left with an open ending, the House in which Fear and Pathos reign.

Another note on the prosody of *B:* there are three late stanzas which carry six lines each, and rime-pattern *abbaab*. It is frequent in the sestets of Italianate sonnets, though their lines keep to their five-beat measure. The husband speaks the first of these stanzas, which contains all the matter of the final *A* stanza, and a little more, as we have just seen. But the friend takes two stanzas, first to counsel the husband to patience with his bride, and then to advise him that she seems not to be a proper poet, and may exercise her right of truancy again. The friend is evidently older than the husband, and more severe with poets who do not conform to the tradition. He is a little quaint, too, in his forms of speech.

Conrad Sits in Twilight

A

Conrad, Conrad, aren't you old
To sit so late in a mouldy garden?
And I think Conrad knows it well,
Nursing his knees, too rheumy and cold
To warm the wraith of a Forest of Arden.

Neuralgia in the back of his neck,
His lungs filling with such miasma,
His feet dipping in leafage and muck:
Conrad, you've forgotten asthma.

Conrad's house has thick red walls
And chips on Conrad's hearth are blazing,
Slippers and pipe and tea are served,
Anchovy toast, Conrad! 'Tis pleasing,
Still Conrad's back is not uncurved,
And here's an autumn on him, teasing.

Autumn days in our section
Are the most used-up thing on earth,
(Or in the waters under the earth),
Having no more color nor predilection
Than cornstalks too wet for the fire,
A ribbon rotting on the byre,
A man's face as weathered as straw
By the summer's flare and the winter's flaw.

Conrad, rise up, and steel your soul
And smite an anvil, draw a sword
(See William James and Henry Ford)
And point you to a mightier goal!
But Conrad has not answered a word.

The poem was first published in *The Fugitive*, Vol. II, No. 5, Nashville, Tenn., 1924.

The poem is casual in its riming, but without disastrous faults. The final stanza was dropped in later publications; it seemed anticlimactic after the long fourth stanza, which my readers have liked the best. There is an error in its sixth line, where I had taken the "byre" to be the manure-pile by the stable: I have learned from my dictionary that it is the stable itself.

Master's in the Garden Again

B

I

Evening comes early, and soon discovers
Exchange between two conjugate lovers.

"Conrad! dear man, surprise! aren't you bold
To be sitting so late in your sodden garden?"

"Woman! intrusion! does this promise well?
I'm nursing my knees, they are not very cold.
Have you known the fall of a year when it fell?
Indeed it's a garden, but if you will pardon
The health of a garden is somebody's burden."

"Conrad, your feet are dripping in muck,
The neuralgia will settle in your own neck,
And whose health is it that catches an asthma?
Come in from foul weather for pity's sake!"

He is gentle but firm. "Concede, my dear,
I'm warden of garden, and mind its miasma.
If my loony is lonely her house is up there,
Go and wait! If you won't I'll go jump in the lake."

II

And the master's back has not uncurved
Nor the autumn's blow for an instant swerved.

Autumn days in our section
Are the most used-up thing on earth
(Or in the waters under the earth)

Having no more color nor predilection
Than a man's face as weathered as straw
By summer's flare and autumn's flaw,
Or cornstalks too wet for the fire,
Or rain of leaves that writhe in the mire.

The leaves are all dead. There is no defection.

III

By the breath of the Power the dark skies lower,
By the bite of Its frost the children were lost
Who hurt no one where they shone in the sun,
But the valiant heart knows a better part
Than to do with an "O did It lay them low,
But we're a poor sinner just going to dinner."

See the tell-tale art of the champion heart.

Here's temple and brow which frown like the law,
If the arm lies low yet the rage looks high,
The accusing eye is a fierce round O!
The offense was raw, says the stubborn jaw,
We'll raise a big row and heave a hard blow,
And let's do it now!

A pantomime blow, if it damned him to do,
A yell mumming too. But it's gay garden now,
Play sweeter than pray, that the darkened be gay.

Here is a man who has done what he can,
Now he will defer to the house and to her.

COMMENT

My head was full of rime when I wrote this poem; a tiny composition with three movements, all different, but coming finally to terms

with each other. First is the exchange between Conrad and his wife, a pair of vocalists whose duet is won by the master of the garden. Next is the sad and brooding movement when the ravenous autumn has stripped the leaves from the trees. Finally comes Conrad's furious onslaught against the hateful deity who has accomplished it; though he can manage it only in pantomime. In the conclusion of that movement the author speaks for him, congratulating him equally for the happiness of his poetic imagination, and the temporizing peace which returns him to his daily round of duties.

The *B* poem was first printed in my *Selected Poems*, Alfred A. Knopf, 1963; then in the final volume of the series called *New World Writing*, J. B. Lippincott, Philadelphia, 1964. The second printing did not stand by itself; the arrangement which contained it consisted of five parts: first the new poem, then three critical essays by as many reputable poet-critics, and finally the poet's reply to them. The set in which my poem figured was in the same pattern as the other sets already completed. The originator of this excellent scheme was Anthony Ostroff, of the University of California at Berkeley. He was responsible for eight such collections, which in 1964 he published in a single book, *The Contemporary Poet as Artist and Critic*, Little, Brown & Co., Boston and Toronto. It is very nearly a "must" for a poet's reading. I am grateful to him for the mere fragments of my final essay which I give here; and sorry that there is no room at all for excerpts from my poet-critics' essays.

The present poem is a revision of the *B* poem of 1963 and 1964; two degrees removed from the original *A*. My critics changed my mind in some respects. There was some accusation of Conrad's brutal language to the wife who had come to rescue him from the bitter weather. For example, the naughty man means to hear out her unrimed lines, then cap them in his reply with a group of lines that supply rime-mates for her lines, and for good measure some rimes of his own. That is why her first address in two lines ending with *bold* and *garden* is followed by his stanza of five lines ending with *well*, *cold*, *fell*, *pardon*, *burden;* two separate rimes for her *garden*. Her next sally has four lines ending with *muck*, *neck*, *asthma*, and *sake*. His reply is to assume that *muck* and *neck* may be put to her credit as lame rimes (a little of his art having rubbed off on her) though probably their near-riming is wholly accidental. He replies with four lines ending with *hear*, *miasma*, *there*, and *lake*. If his replies seem insulting, it could be one of their conventions in arguing; for she is not strictly a singer, though her diction is excellent. In any event, I took the poet-critics' objections to heart and "sweetened" Conrad's final stanza; though I had felt that the tone and manner of their talking was largely persiflage and convention between them. And I was obliged to think that she did not finally leave the garden because of his threat to "jump in the lake"; she had no fear of his doing that, and knew the phrase only as his way of turning off an argument.

The second movement required a little revision too, especially in respect to the last line, which stands apart from the big stanza but ends with a rime which chimes exactly with that of two important lines above. My critics had thought that the lamentation of the movement was dealing with the general mortality, including our own, and everybody's; but the final line declares the real topic as the fallen leaves.

That topic is worked over in the final movement. Conrad denounces the Power, the "It" itself, which has committed these million murders. Here we are obliged to observe that Conrad is of the same theological persuasion as the early Thomas Hardy, who made many ferocious onslaughts against the deity on the very same ground, and gave him the name of "It" because the creature had not yet acquired the moral sense that belongs to man. The best evidence of Hardy's early attitude is in the enormous epic drama *The Dynasts*, where he was of the same persuasion as Conrad. I have a special fondness for Hardy's verse. But for the sake of Conrad, the hero in the present action, I have removed the dedication to Thomas Hardy. I have not changed the title, which surely derives from Hardy's little poem "The Master and the Leaves," 1917. There the leaves are complaining of their streaks of color, which means, as they know, their death-warrant. But at this date the Master cannot comfort them, because he now embraces the philosophy of the Immanent Presence, who disposes the action of his creatures toward evil as well as good, in order to ensure their vitality as long as they last. I cannot deny that my imagination, in which one image seems to suggest another, would easily picture Mr. T. H. drooping on a cold metal chair in a prospect of fallen leaves, and maintaining his posture with slightest variations while he brooded over many things. He must often have sat in his garden, and his mind was active till he died in his eighty-eighth year. But my version of Hardy in the garden was a fleeting vision which I could not verify as a mere image because it was likely to have been a historic truth.

There remains for discussion only the peculiar prosody of the third movement. Each line has four beats, of which the second and fourth must rime together. With this rule existing, it is possible to isolate a whole line, such as the one standing after the opening passage; it conforms to the rule. But in the third and fourth passages, which contain eight and a half lines, there are but six separate base-rimes. These find their partners anywhere they can and please; for that rule I presume, properly and historically as I think, that even two different rimes in the same line having open vowel-endings are legitimate rime-partners. (We may have open vowels followed by a silent letter or letters, but that makes no difference.) The original rime-words number seventeen, and occur first in the following order: *brow, law, low, high, do, pray.* Seventeen rimes with six key-rimes! The passage is brisk indeed; or should I say "brusque"? It seems to fit the occasion. My critics either disliked the rime-scheme or ignored it, and I do not blame them. In the present form I have done away with the middle stops at least in the third part, except in one line, and made the "tell-tale art of the champion heart" take on a sort of grace in showing the disfigurement of the sitter's features.

And now as to the fourth stanza, and the admonition to the champion in the final couplet. The blow was "pantomime," says the speaker, and the yell was "mumming." But he is pleased with this miming, and congratulates Conrad for having attained to a very honest and earned aesthetic posture. I believe with him that the imagination succeeds with a fiction when the real or desired action is impossible; it put me on the track of a fresh understanding of the policies of poetry. There is religion in it, too; perhaps just as much as there is in prayer. We are ready now for the final dismissal of Conrad, who must return to the daily round of living.

Agitato ma non troppo

A

I have a grief,
(It was not stolen like a thief),
Albeit I have no bittern by the lake
To cry it up and down the brake.

There hath been none like Dante's fury
When Beatrice was given him to bury;
Except, when the young heart was hit, you know
How Percy Shelley's reed sang tremolo.

"If grief be in his mind,
Where is his Fair Child moaning in the wind?
Where is the whitefrost snowing on his head?
When did he stalk and weep and not loll in his bed?"

I will be brief,
Assuredly I have a grief
And I am shaken; but not as a leaf.

COMMENT

The *A* poem was first published in *The Fugitive*, Vol. II, No. 5, 1923. I note several errors of form or fact. The comma after the parenthesis in stanza one is superfluous. Beatrice was not given to Dante to bury; his passion for her began with their meeting when each was nine years old, but she married another man and died at the age of twenty-five. The "Albeit" of the first stanza and the "hath" of the second seem a little quaint nowadays. Finally, the reader is disturbed in stanza three by the phrase "the whitefrost snowing on," which is hardly logical.

In title and argument, as well as over-all shape, the *B* poem will resemble *A*, but it will have a larger and stricter development. I meant in these poems to plead for modesty and moderation in our griefs for the death of relatives and friends; and against the frantic outcries and lamentations which suggest the behavior of the wild romantics, whether in fact or verse. F. O. Mathiessen, in his book about American verse, commended my principle. But I was becoming sensitive over the death-frequencies of my poems.

III   Agitato ma non troppo

B

This is what the man said,
Insisting, standing on his head.

Yes, I have come to grief,
It was not furtive like a thief,
And must not be blown up beyond belief.

They know I have no bittern by the lake
To cry it up and down the brake,
And nothing since has been like Dante's fury
For Beatrice who was not his to bury,
Except, if the young heart faltered, they may know
How Shelley's throbbing reed sang tremolo.

They say, "He puts a fix upon his mind,
And hears at bedside or in the moaning wind
The rumor of Death; yet he can't mount one tear
But stalks with holy calm beside the terrible bier."

Lest we wreck upon a reef,
I go according to another brief,
Against their killing blasts of grief.

My head, outposted promontoried chief,
Frowned, and elected me to the common grief,
By whose poor pities I'm shaken, but not as a leaf.

COMMENT

Readers of poetry, I believe, know that the ecstasy of verse depends in
the first place upon its aural dimension, that consists chiefly in the

formal beauty of its rhythm or measure; then in the rime-endings if they are provided; and finally in the delicious play among the consonants chiming sweetly and unexpectedly from phrase to phrase, and likewise among the vowels.

But I am impelled to propose a second dimension, which resides in the poem's visual form. It exhibits an artful and spatial design upon the flat plane of the paper. I believe that nowadays we acquaint ourselves with a poem not by hearing or reciting it, but by seeing and reading it silently. In our tradition it was George Herbert who first shaped his poems into symmetrical and various forms; for example in the famous "Easter Wings," where the placement of the first and last letters of the individual lines was meant to outline the four wings of two larks who sang out of their heavenly joy just as the poet liked to do. Only once do I recall seeing the "Wings" precisely outlined, but it was at the expense of horrid gaps within some of the lines. The failure of his designs disheartens his devotees; we can only imagine the careful and beautiful patterns which he may have completed in his script. He died at the age of thirty, before he could turn them over to the printer. But speaking generally, it astonishes me that I can hardly find a single stanza, of as few as half a dozen lines, set up in a perfect rectangular block; though I have looked deep into the huge volumes of certain anthologists. Perhaps every worthy stanza ever written by a good poet has aspired to the dignity of perfect printed form. But the printer sticks to his trade. In any case let it be said that the authentic sense of visual verse-form has no correspondent in prose; or in the impromptu and irregular lengths of line which many otherwise good poets practice today.

Let me now define the visual-mathematical form of the stanzas of *B*. The vertical on the left boundary is as sturdy as can be; and so are the horizontals which take off to the right. But the horizontals of each stanza lengthen progressively and equally as they go; so that their end-points describe a line which slopes sharply downward from the horizontal. The angles seem equal; they are at least approximately equal; so that the sloping lines throughout the poem are parallel.

There is one extra feature. In the third stanza, lines one, three, and five are longer respectively than lines two, four, and six; but the slope of the shorter lines keeps the angle of departure from the horizontal and defines a line parallel to, but inside, the outer slope.

But what does the spatial pattern of the poem symbolize to the reader? Let me suppose a customer who is not interested in the moral or philosophical sense of the poem, but has a great affection for flower gardens. The form of the poem suggests to him, let us say, a biggish garden, containing six separate flower-plots. If I were younger and stronger, I would have pleasure in making and tending it. I would fill the rows of the separate plots with flowers to my liking; and very congenial would be the well-clipped horizontal turfs between adjacent plots to walk upon. But I would replace the end-flowers of the two central plots with ten plants of Burpee's Climax Marigold, which bear blazing orange flowers; and the end-flowers of the upper and lower plots with Wayside Gardens' Aster Frikarti, whose blossoms are bright lavender. Both varieties bloom constantly in the summer season, and are of suitable size. Think how the farmer and the visitors would be intrigued by the displacements of the sloping front border, which do not subtract a foot from its lawful length.

But now to reckon with a more important symbol than a garden and its visual design. After the speaker and his critics have finished fighting, the two final stanzas must be enforced; they make the proper conclusion. The speaker denounces the "killing blasts of grief" which "they" utter on painful and mortal occasions. He has good authority: his mentor is defined in the first stanza of the poem, and is exactly described in the final stanza. The poem is best symbolized not by its shape on the paper, but by the morality and social sense of the meanings of the words.

I V Tom, Tom, the Piper's Son

A

Grim in my little black coat as the sleazy beetle,
And gone of hue,
Lonely, a man reputed for softening little,
Loving few—

Mournfully going where men assemble, unfriended, pushing
To sell my wares,
And glaring with little grey eyes at whom I am brushing,
Who would with theirs—

Full of my thoughts as I trudge here and trundle yonder,
Eyes on the ground,
Tricked by white birds or tall women into no wonder
And no sound—

Yet privy to great dreams, and secret in vainglory.
And hot and proud,
And poor and bewildered, and longing to hear my own story
Rehearsed aloud—

How I have passed, involved in these chances and choices,
By certain trees
Whose tiny attent auricles receive the true voices
Of the wordless breeze—

And against me the councils of spirits were not then darkened
Who thereby house,
As I set my boots to the path beneath them, and harkened
To the talking boughs—

How one said, "This ambulant worm, he is strangely other
Than they suppose"—

But one, "He was sired by his father and dammed by his mother
And acknowledges those"—

And then: "Nay, nay—this man is a changeling, and knows not—
This was a Prince
From a far great kingdom—and should return, but goes not—
Long years since"—

But like a King I was subject to a King's condition,
And I marched on,
Not testing at eavesdrop the glory of my suspicion,
And the talkers were gone—

And duly appeared I on the very clock-throb appointed
In the litten room,
Nor was hailed with that love that leaps to the Heir Anointed:
"Hush, hush, he is come!"

COMMENT

This poem was published originally in *The Fugitive*, Vol. III, No. 6, 1924. It is not too bad a poem for publication, but a painful one which ends without any resolution of Tom's final despair. Musically, the short two-foot line which follows the long pentameter above it gives us something of a jolt. And in terms of punctuation, we wonder about the many dashes which close all the stanzas except the final one; I do not think it was prompted by the habit of Emily Dickinson's style, but rather that it seemed suitable to the speaker to continue his weary and unprofitable stanzas with dashes which indicate the doggedness of his search, till the very last stanza disposes of all his dashes and hopes together. I think he might have excluded his second stanza, where Tom seems to characterize himself as a Fuller Brush man, or some other kind of door-to-door salesman.

IV The Vanity of the Bright Boys

B

Absurd in his tight black coat like a sleazy beetle
He wasn't minding his looks,
He looked inside, at the boy bereaved of his title
Minding his dreams and books.

To assembly he walked alone, but forever pushing
Even to say his prayers,
Glaring with coldest eyes at whom he was brushing
Who could, if they would, with theirs.

In late afternoons he walked in a green fable
And wasted for his miracle,
Should a yellow beak intone from a throat of sable
One syllable of his Oracle.

Even walking he dreamed; and partial in his choices
He called on the Druid trees,
Dark gods whose leaves translated the judgment voices
Stitched in the wind's wheeze;

He shortened stride at a shrubbery where two together
Parleyed, and question rose:

One saying, "The boy who tugs at tether may be other
Than he and they suppose."
But one, "Yet sired and dammed by a father and mother
And you have record of those?"

"That sweet babe royal, if he was changed unknowing
Though still he plays the Prince—"
"A King to be? With his sword and crest not showing?"
"Fifteen long winters since—"

He awoke, ashamed, absolved of brain-washed ambition
And tired royal blood;

Of malingering Prince, from whose vegetary operation
He sprang to his ravening stride—

Stopping eavesdropping for wavering name and nation
From wrangling ghosts and wide—

To see if he throve where the tower's last throb expired
And was dumb in the unlistening room
And the babble of boys. O if they'd stared and adored
Crying "Look, hush, he has come!"

No; but they waved a welcome to bright boy returning
As blest for having him there,
Who laughed and sat; with only an instant's mourning
For castles in the air.

The evening's orator rose to his height of speaking
And wantoned with Heaven and Doom;
The boy indifferent; all that long Night of Waking
Addressing his blessings at home.

L'ENVOI

Dawn, you've purpled a politic Prince,
He's done no running and peeking since,
Thrones are trash, and Kings are dumb,
Say, would he rather his kingdom come?

COMMENT

I came very early to detest the *A* poem for its faults, which would
never have done for my present title about the "bright boys." One

revision appeared in the second edition of my *Selected Poems* in 1963. It was not too bad, but the hateful ending is still there, the hero has no foreseeable future. The final and radical revision is the present *B* poem. But it is rather terse, and heavy with sentiments and by-plays.

Prosodically speaking, I have removed the marks of punctuation at the ends of the long lines (except in the exchanges of the two speakers in stanzas six and seven), and lengthened the two beats of the following short lines to three beats, to make each time one single flowing sentence of two lines.

The boy of the narrative is not the vagabond "Tom, Tom," of the *A* version, but nameless; only a very special sample of the "bright boys" as a school. At fourteen years I can remember having had some notion of the possibility that I had lost a kingdom somewhere, but I did not take off for the roads and hills at any time to find it; nor did any other schoolboy that I knew. The theme of the changeling Prince is an ancient one, and at our Latin Academy it excited us.

There are four additions to the substance of the *A* narrative. I was at pains to show that the hero was a schoolboy, though *A* never mentions or implies it. In *B's* first two stanzas he appears clearly; and in stanza eleven the bell of the tower strikes the hour, the boys have assembled to hear a speaker's address, and our boy arrives just in time. Next, I have interposed after the first two stanzas a fresh one about the bird whose croaking seems to the boy his Oracle trying vainly to tell him where his lost kingdom lies. Then, there are two stanzas just below the final stanzas of the *A* version that show how the other boys waved a welcome to their bright boy, so that his wish is gratified and not nullified. Lastly, in the final stanza, the "evening's orator" utters his profundities, to which the boy does not listen, because now and in all that "Night of Waking" he is planning his own future, and very properly.

Following the text of the narrative, there is a stanza written by the author a few days later in the form of an *envoi;* an old-fashioned address by the author to his patroness, the Dawn Goddess, whom he thanks for having "purpled a politic Prince." It is a short stanza, but he has time to say that the bright boy has "done no running and peeking since"; and to conclude by asking her if the boy means for his kingdom to "come" rather than his looking for it ready-made. It is a rhetorical question which is not answered by the Goddess, but he assumes her affirmative reply. We are left wondering only what sort of kingdom it will be: political, scientific, scholarly? Is there a chance that it will be some revered kingdom of art, such as theater, or music, or verse? That remains for the bright boy to determine.

Semi-Centennial

A

When the green army battled and drove North
The black army, one old fugitive crept forth
From his hole beside the hearth, wearied a little
With fixing his blue eye on ash and spittle.

He hopped outdoors stiff-legged on his stave
To quiz the spring and see if it would grave
Bright images on a mind so weathered and hard
It scarcely received the print of his backyard.

He was a small man with head larger than most,
And so much it had kept, and so much lost,
It could not buzz and spin with giddy mirth
At these quick salad hues that gauded earth.

Business brighter than that had been enacted
Day after day within the curled compacted
Grey hemispheres—music and histories
Enveloping more than April novelties.

If the grey cloud of thought for once was stilled
For the green cycle fifty times fulfilled,
Yet it was feathers that quivered, grass, the bee,
The foal, the firstling yellow bloom—not he.

He leaned upon the earth and turned his eyes
About the world and said with no surprise—
"I am a god. I may not seem to be,
The other gods have disinherited me.

"The better part of godhead is design.
This is not theirs only, for I know mine,

And I project such worlds as need not yield
To this commanded April in the field.

"And it is ample. For it satisfies
My royal blood even thus to exercise
The ancestral arts of my theogony.
I am a god though none attends to me."

And he watched, with large head resting in the sun,
The gods at play, and did not envy one.
He had the magic too, and knew his power,
But was too tired to work it at this hour.

COMMENT

This poem was printed originally in *The Fugitive*, Vol. IV, No. 2,
1925. But some years after the *Fugitive* group dispersed our good
and knowing historian made a very full history of the members and of
their individual poems in the magazine. I will take the liberty to use
Louise Cowan's comment on this poem.

In this poem, an old man, exiled from the physical world for fifty years,
comes out to view the spring, which turns out to be less exciting to him
than the "music and histories" which made up his interior life. He knows
himself a god because of his ability to design large schemes, though he
recognizes his lack of power to execute them. Nature will not obey him, in
his "poverty and disrepute." . . . Composed just before the Vanderbilt
Semi-Centennial celebration, the poem can be read as delineating the
powerless yet withal superior position of the university in relation to the
actual world of action. The old man's is the philosophical position Ransom
condemned in his first volume, particularly in "The Swimmers," and it is
the position shown throughout his poems to be fatally wrong, though
eternally desirable.

The only amendment I would make to this account is that the fifty
years of the old man's exile from the world of affairs were hardly the
whole years of his life; his exile had begun at the age when he took to
the life of the imagination and followed it faithfully; let us say, at the
age of twenty-five. His Semi-Centennial birthday, however, coincided
with that of the university.

Birthday of an Aging Seer

(*b. June 24, 1865*)

B

When the green army drove the black one North,
An overwintered seer came smiling forth
From hearth whereof the stain of ash and spittle
Compounded with his thought, which was not little.

Outdoors he hopped stiff-legged on his stave
To quiz the spring and see if it would grave
Fresh images on a screen so brightly starred
It scarcely took the print of his backyard.

That sexagenarian head we worship almost,
For so much it had kept, and so much lost,
It could not loud applaud the laboring earth
For hatching another salad brood to birth.

Business better than that had been enacted,
Year in and out, within the curled compacted
Grey hemispheres; love dreams, and histories
Brisker even than springtime novelties.

If the wide wave of thought for once was stilled
For his annual cycle a sixtieth time fulfilled,
It was bird-feather that quivered, grass, the bee,
The foal, the darling yellow bloom, not he.

He leaned upon the earth, he lifted eyes
Unto the heavens, and said with no surprise:

"I am a god transcending things that be,
And the proper gods have disinherited me.

"Such is the parsimony of proper god,
Illiterate nature minds, if he but nod;
But with my power, and thriving on disrepute,
I speak, and pure souls hear and execute.

"The better part of godhood is design.
If other gods have theirs, then leave me mine,
For I compose such worlds as do not yield
To that commanded pageant of the field.

"My worlds are Irish, and it satisfies
The Irish folk that I should exercise
The ancestral arts of their theogony.
I am their god, and they depend on me."

COMMENT

The *B* poem keeps the philosophy which Miss Cowan has explained. But now it is fortified by finding a historic person to replace the nameless old man of *A*.

The *A* poem now seems very much tangled in ambiguities. I was writing only about a possible but unknown fifty-year-old philosopher-hero or artist-hero for the sake of the Vanderbilt Semi-Centennial. Only now has it startled me to recognize him as a real person, whose birthday fell on June 24. But the year 1925 had his sixtieth birthday! The poem comes to life. As to the man's divinity, the Unknown God has implanted in him that special degree of godhood which consists in the freedom of the æsthetic imagination. Few persons have received that gratuity in such measure as to require them to adopt the life of artists. But this one did, and had his meed of fame.

The added final stanza tells us that he was an Irishman. I must tease my readers a little by withholding his name. The good readers will know him.

VI Here Lies a Lady

A

Here lies a lady of beauty and high degree.
Of chills and fever she died, of fever and chills,
The delight of her husband, her aunt, an infant of three,
And of medicos marveling sweetly on her ills.

For either she burned, and her confident eyes would blaze,
And her fingers fly in a manner to puzzle their heads—
What was she making? Why, nothing; she sat in a maze
Of old scraps of laces, snipped into curious shreds—

Or this would pass, and the light of her fire decline
Till she lay discouraged and cold, like a thin stalk white and blown,
And would not open her eyes, to kisses, to wine;
The sixth of these states was her last; the cold settled down.

Sweet ladies, long may ye bloom, and toughly I hope ye may thole,
But was she not lucky? In flowers and lace and mourning,
In love and great honor we bade God rest her soul
After six little spaces of chill, and six of burning.

COMMENT

The poem was first published in my *Poems and Essays*, Vintage edition, 1945. The *B* poem will follow, and its lines correspond so closely to the *A* lines that I need not detail the better phrases of *B*. But I must note that the second line of stanza three here is a hexameter instead of the standard pentameter of the poem, and contains a very dubious phrase, "like a thin stalk white and blown," which hardly describes the image of a beautiful woman even in her ravage. In stanza four the first line is another hexameter; and the archaic "ye" may be a little too quaint.

Here Lies a Lady

B

Here lies a lady of beauty and high degree,
Of chills and fever she died, of fever and chills,
The delight of her husband, an aunt, an infant of three
And medicos marveling sweetly on her ills.

First she was hot, and her brightest eyes would blaze
And the speed of her flying fingers shook their heads.
What was she making? God knows; she sat in those days
With her newest gowns all torn, or snipt into shreds.

But that would pass, and the fire of her cheeks decline
Till she lay dishonored and wan like a rose overblown,
And would not open her eyes, to kisses, to wine;
The sixth of which states was final. The cold came down.

Fair ladies, long may you bloom, and sweetly may thole!
She was part lucky. With flowers and lace and mourning,
With love and bravado, we bade God rest her soul
After six quick turns of quaking, six of burning.

COMMENT

The opening stanzas of *A* and *B* are alike; in the later stanzas *B* is far
superior. The second stanza has the lady sitting among her newest
gowns and destroying them; but there may be two interpretations.
She may be planning to get a new wardrobe when she has recovered
from her illness. That seems at first the sign of a great lady's vanity:
why is she not talking with her husband and her child? (The aunt
may be hundreds of miles away.) But she must occupy herself
somehow while she can; and the husband is a wealthy and busy man,

who cannot attend her at all times, while her child is forbidden her bedside. The third stanza, where chill replaces fever, is almost unutterably painful; but I was most intent upon it, and managed to the best of my ability. Lines two and three are the saddest in the poem; perhaps in all my poems. Line two has her lying "dishonored and wan like a rose overblown," where the two phrases almost rime. Line three has her at the very point of death; and line four announces the ultimate fact. In stanza four the only thing the friends and relatives can do is to bring their tokens of affection to the coffin; but these are supplemented in line three with "love and bravado" when they ask God to "rest her soul." The "bravado" may seem strange; until we reflect that any prayer has that constituent, inasmuch as it is addressed to an Unknown God whose designs we cannot thwart. The final line is new and fresh after the twenty-odd years' service of the *A* line. And lines three and four together supply, I suppose, two reasons why she was "part lucky"; first because of the devotion of her loyal subjects, and then because of the brevity of her illness.

Of Margaret

A

With the fall of the first leaf that winds rend
She and the boughs trembled, and she would mourn
The wafer body as an own first-born,
But with louder destruction sang the wind.

Soon must they all descend, there where they hung
In gelid air, and the blind land be filled
With dead, and a mere windiness unchild
Her of the sons of all her mothering.

No mother sorrow is but follows birth,
And, beyond that, conception; hers was large,
And so immoderate love must be a scourge,
Needing the whole ecstasy of substant earth.

But no evil shall spot this, Margaret's page,
For her generations were of the head,
The eyes, the tender fingers, not the blood,
And the issue was all flowers and foliage.

Virgin, whose image bent to the small grass
I keep against this tide of wayfaring,
O hear the maiden pageant ever sing
Of that far away time of gentleness.

COMMENT

The poem was first printed in ~~my~~ *Poems and Essays,* ~~Vintage edition,~~ a magazine
~~1945.~~ I thought well of it, and it has been anthologized and has
pleased readers who have spoken or written to me. But just now I feel

that it is an unusually good specimen of an *A* poem and not a *B* poem. I do not find very great faults in it. But it needs no explication, and I think we had better go at once to the *B* version.

Of Margaret

B

Frost, and a leaf has quit the tulip tree
Wafting on brightest airs with twist and turn;
The wafer body is Margaret's first-born.
A day of dark shall be her Calvary.

Then shall the leaves be stained with weathering,
And the green sward of a sudden be defiled
With surfeit, till one soft wind of grace unchild
Her of the sons of all her mothering.

No mother sorrow is but follows birth,
And beyond that, conception; hers was large,
And so immoderate love must be a scourge
Needing the whole ecstasy of substant earth.

But no evil shall spot this, Margaret's page.
The generations born of her loving mood
Were modes of yellow greenery, not of blood,
And the faithful issue was blossom and foliage.

Virgin, whose bravest image in the grass
I keep against this tide of wayfaring,
O hear the maiden pageant ever sing
Of that far away time of gentleness.

COMMENT

The very first word of the poem is "Frost," which is the keyword of its stanza, followed by the fall of the first leaf of the tulip tree and its brilliant but hopeless descent to earth. But the last line of the stanza likens the virgin Margaret to the Holy Mary whose Son had died on the tree of Calvary.

In stanza two all the leaves must die, and there are four foul words which set the tone of the passage: "stained," "defiled," "surfeit," and "unchild." But there is a beautiful recovery when "one soft wind of grace" hastens the universal fall of the leaves.

Stanza three argues like a physiologist against the innumerable "conceptions" by the virgin Margaret. It is a replica of the *A* version, and doubtless *A*'s best stanza, except for the last, of which the *B* stanza is again a replica, with only one slight change.

Stanza four of *B*'s version replies to the argument of stanza three, and is much less physical. Margaret's innumerable conceptions were of leaves, not of human babes. But there is something as innocent and magical in Margaret as a fairy godmother, bringing gifts of "blossom and foliage" to the earth people.

But in my limited repertory I could never find a lovelier conclusion than the stanza five which finishes this poem. Nor a more moving one; it is pure elegy, uttered by an old "wayfaring" fellow, who addresses the lost virgin of his younger days. What he asks of her is wonderful but impossible. He wants her to hear the "maiden pageant" who at his instance will sing forever of that "far away time of gentleness."

At my age I do not mind at this point making a few personal remarks. During the *Fugitive* days of my fourth decade I was at great pains to suppress my feelings in what I wrote. I was both sensitive and sentimental as a boy; and I did not like that boyishness in my adult poems. My friends seemed to think that I managed it. But here I take pleasure in testifying that I could not easily control my feelings when I was finishing two very special poems, which stand here side by side by virtue of their dates: they are "Here Lies a Lady" and "Of Margaret," in the *B* versions. These are the poems which, as I finished them, wetted my cheeks. But I must add that they are fictions.

VIII   Prelude to an Evening

A

Do not enforce the tired wolf
Dragging his infected wound homeward
To sit tonight with the warm children
Naming the pretty kings of France.

The images of the invaded mind
Being as monsters in the dreams
Of your most brief enchanted headful,
Suppose a miracle of confusion:

That dreamed and undreamt become each other
And mix the night and day of your mind;
And it does not matter your twice crying
From mouth unbeautied against the pillow

To avert the gun of the swarthy soldier,
For cry, cock-crow, or the iron bell
Can crack the sleep-sense of outrage,
Annihilate phantoms who were nothing.

But now, by our perverse supposal,
There is a drift of fog on your mornings;
You in your peignoir, dainty at your orange-cup,
Feel poising round the sunny room

Invisible evil, deprived, and bold.
All day the clock will metronome
Your gallant fear; the needles clicking,
The heels detonating the stair's cavern.

Freshening the water in the blue bowls
For the buckberries with not all your love,

You shall be listening for the low wind,
The warning sibilance of pines.

You like a waning moon, and I accusing
Our too banded Eumenides,
You shall make Noes but wanderingly,
Smoothing the heads of the hungry children.

COMMENT

Poem *A* was published in the *American Review* of April 1934. Its eight stanzas stood without change in the *Selected Poems* and the Vintage edition of ~~1945~~ *1955*. It became a subsidiary, or *A*, poem only near the end of *Selected Poems*, 1963, when its length was increased by five stanzas and a long Comment full of Biblical lore and morals. The social issue is saved, but I, like some of my friends, am not sure whether an expiation is always in the interest of a fiction. The *B* Comment is given in full.

VIII Prelude to an Evening

B

Do not enforce the tired wolf
Dragging his infected wound homeward
To sit tonight with the warm children
Saying the pretty Kings of France.

You are my scholar. Then languish, expire,
With each day's terror and next week's doom,
Till we're twice espoused, in love and ruin,
And grave but smiling as the heavens fall.

The images of the invaded mind
Were monstrous only in the dreams
Of your most brief enchanted headful.
Suppose a miracle of confusion: —

That dreamed and undreamt become each other
And mix the night and day of your soul.
For it never mattered your twice crying
From mouth unbeautied against the pillow

To avert the gun of the same old soldier,
If quickly cry, cock-crow or bell
Breaking the dark improbable spell
Annihilated the poor phantom.

And now? To confirm our strange supposal,
Your monsters wait upon sunniest mornings;
You in your peignoir put marvels of oranges
Gold on the platter for cheeky children

But freeze at the turbulence under the floor
Where unclean spirits yawn and thrash;

The day-long clock will strike your fears;
The heels detonating the stair's cavern.

Freshening the water in the blue bowls
For the buckberries with not all your love
You listen for another wind to waken
The sibilant warning of sentinel pines.

Finally evening. Hear me denouncing
Our equal and conniving Furies;
You making Noes but they lack conviction;
Smoothing the heads of the hungry children.

I would have us magnificent at my coming,
Two souls tight-clasped, in a swamp of horrors,
But you shall be handsome and brave at fearing.
Now my step quickens—and meets a huge No!

Whose No was it, like the hoarse policeman's,
Clopping on stage in the Name of the Law?
That was me, forbidding tricks at homecoming
Just as I'm nearing the white threshold.

I have gone to the nations of disorder
To be quit of the memory of good and evil;
There even your image was disfigured,
But the boulevards rocked; they said, Go back.

I am here; and to balk my ruffian I bite
The tongue rehearsing all that treason;
Then stride in my wounds to the sovereign flare
Of the room where you shine on the good children.

"Prelude to an Evening," in thirteen stanzas, is a new version of the original poem by that title, which had eight stanzas and was published thirty years ago. In the new poem the eight stanzas remain substantially about what they were before. The big change is the addition of four new stanzas at the end. They are like the others in form, being quatrains of unrimed four-beat lines which mostly are end-stopped. It was my hope that the new stanzas would be like enough in tempo and style to keep continuity with the old ones as if by a single act of composition. But I am afraid that these so new and so few stanzas, doing so much in so short space, may be too brisk to suit with the others. What they must do is nothing less than undo the whole intention of the old poem, and bring it to a very different conclusion. Besides these four new stanzas there is another which makes a second stanza within the original eight. I wanted to define more sharply the situation which seemed to call for a reversal; now it takes nine stanzas, and has to be reversed in four.

Several friends have asked me why I thought I must change the ending so radically. The simple fact is that it became disagreeable to my ears as I continued to read it on public occasions now and then.

Here is a man returning in the evening from his worldly occupations to his own household. He has had plenty of encounters with the world's evils, and his imagination is immoderate and wayward; it has blown the evils up, till now he manages to be attended habitually by a vague but overwhelming impression of metaphysical Powers arrayed against him; he can say even to others (if they are capable of sympathy) that he is a man pursued by Furies. And he cannot but think it an anticlimax, a defeat unworthy of his confrontation of his fate, to spend the evening with children at their lessons. The poem is the man's soliloquy as he approaches his house. He is addressing the mother of his children, who awaits him, as if rehearsing the speech he will make in her presence in order to persuade her to share his fearful preoccupations and give him her entire allegiance. He seems to think he will win her over; there is no intimation that it may turn out quite differently. But suppose he succeeds: will not that be a dreary fate for the woman? And what of the children? Those are not his questions. But they came to be mine. By the end of the ninth stanza he pictures her prophetically as rapt in her new terrors, almost to the point of forgetting the children; if they are hungry, she will absent-mindedly smooth their heads.

I suppose a poet is excused without having to invoke the Fifth Amendment if he believes in his own poem, at least at the stage of first publication. My liking went quite beyond its merits, and lasted much too long. It had to do with some notion of a workmanlike poetic line carrying forward the argument while the woman was being borne through successive terrors not of her own making, yet still invested in her incorruptible dignity. It was with intense pleasure that I watched her suffering there; she was a heroine almost after the pattern of some diminutive classical tragedy. And if the piece had a hero, it must be the husband and speaker. I had not come to saying that the man was odious, that he was, incontestably, the villain. That was rather strange. As for my ordinary conscience in these matters, I believe I have only one other poem so vindictive as this, and I know some readers to whom it is no secret which it must be. It is the one called "Blue Girls," where the girls in the schoolyard are preening themselves in their beauty (as they should) till a man looking on addresses them and forces them to take account of a blear-eyed old woman whom he invents on the spot, and describes, with the threat that to her favor they must come soon.

At any rate, one day last winter, what I had not said was said for me, by a strong-minded young woman writing in a very little magazine devoted to the "explication" of difficult verse, in answer to a subscriber's query. What did the man of my poem mean to do? She replied with a commendable severity: this man was simply a brutal character who meant not to do any baby-sitting even if the babies were his own. At once I conceded the justice of her observation, and with more relief than surprise. All the same, I was soon wondering if I might not somehow patch up the poem and save it; by saving the woman and the children from their distress; and of course by saving the villain too, who so far as the genders go belonged to my party. I rather thought not. If I must administer to him a speedy and radical "conversion" after many stanzas of villainy—the idea was too forbidding.

Another event brought me back to my project of salvage. Twelve years ago Charles Coffin, my teaching colleague, died at the Huntington Library in the midst of his studies of the theology of *Paradise*

Lost. Now Milton had notoriously been a sort of independent theologian; but I was aware that Dr. Coffin, for all his churchmanship, inclined to be an independent theologian too. Unfortunately his packed notebooks were far from complete. But a faithful pupil rescued one complete section or chapter under the title of "Creation and the Self," which he submitted to *ELH* (*A Journal of English Literary History*); it was published in March 1962. The essay might have been the key chapter of the book. It deals first with the magnanimous creation of man in the Creator's image, and then with the man's adventurous behaviors as they affected his relations with the Creator. We must remember that the writer was exploring the mind of Milton, and limiting his speculation scrupulously to the theological ideas that were feasible at the date of Milton's poem. Milton's theme, said Dr. Coffin, is the story of the friendly association between Creator and creature; it is broken many times by the creature's misdemeanors, but the Creator always is prepared to extend his grace; may I remark, though it will be something of an anachronism: as if He had allowed for them in advance? If the creature repents, the happy connection is restored.

I have liked this theology so much for its friendly note that now, and from here on, I will refer symbolically to the man in my poem as Adam, and to the woman whom he apostrophizes as Eve; these are the names they must bear in our Great Myth. In this way I shall not be altogether compromising my poem by "explicating" it. A poem is not a moral essay nor a religious tract; it is best if our talk about it falls short of being just that. We are still feeling the scars of a long, confused period in the modern history of literary criticism in which this issue has been fought over, and perhaps fought out. Poetry is still the supremely inclusive speech which escapes, as if unaware of them, the strictures and reductions of the systematic logical understanding. Publicly or tacitly, we probably all have some sort of theology, and its teachings are quite capable of entering into a poem, perhaps without losing any of their compulsion. It is difficult to write the proper poem nowadays, because after many ages of hard prose we have come far from the primitive and natural speech of poetry. But it is still being handsomely done. In a true poem it is as if the religious dogma or the moral maxim had been dropped into the pot as soon as the act of composition began; sinking down out of sight and consciousness, it is as if it became a fluid and was transfused into the bloodstream of the poet now, and would be communicated to the bloodstream of his auditors eventually. The significance of the poem is received by feeling; or, more technically, by immediate unconscious intuition. So let the man of my poem be Adam, let the woman and mother of his children be Eve; if the poem did not name them, let the commentary do it. At once we are moving over an old and familiar terrain; bearing these names the figures will be invested for everybody with their moral and religious properties.

I cannot fail to remark that I was partly prepared for this symbolic sense of my characters by an event dated 1961: the publication of *The Rhetoric of Religion* by Kenneth Burke; a book which for the largeness of its perspective and the scruple of its discriminations must rate among the important treatises of philosophy. In his foreword Burke remarks:

> The subject of religion falls under the head of *rhetoric* in the sense that rhetoric is the art of *persuasion*, and religious cosmogonies are designed . . . as exceptionally thoroughgoing modes of persuasion. To persuade men towards certain acts, religions would form the kinds of attitude which prepare men for such acts. And in order to plead for such attitudes as persuasively as possible, the religious always ground their exhortations (to themselves and others) in statements of the widest and deepest possible scope, concerning the authorship of men's motives.

A less hortatory form of persuasion, yet a powerful and rhetorical one, is poetry; and it has to be said that Burke as a cunning verbalist has an extraordinary sensibility for the varied meanings that go with a word or phrase. And Burke would think, as I do, that it is more faithful to the sense of a serious poem to translate it into theology, if we must translate it, than into morality. A poem starts with a crucial human situation, and from there proceeds usually by some mixture of drama, narrative, and contemplation. But does not the priest himself teach theology to the congregation most effectively by means of Scriptural narratives and ritualistic drama? The secular-seeming ordinary poem plies its rhetoric through common words, but theology pervades them invisibly. So digressive, and regressive, is the significance of old words even though we may not choose to stop and dwell on them.

But Charles Coffin supplied my most immediate cues. Adam, he said, was the noblest of God's creatures because he was created free; he could choose his own actions. But to guide him he had reason, which was akin to his Creator's; and imagination, so that he might be in his degree a creator in his own right. Imagination is a great term in the Scriptures, but I am afraid that its usual employment there is by way of mention of the evil imaginations of the heart. How prodigious are Adam's creations, even since Milton's time; especially since Milton's time. He has created commodities exactly suited to his physical need, and machines too, to which he has delegated their automatic creation; and terrible engines of war; and as I think we all think increasingly, a foolish clutter of little machines and mechanisms which by saving his strength impoverish it, leaving his body soft and his mind aimless as to its proper objects. He has created gods in his own image, but sometimes they are not flattering to his intelligence, and not fit for universal worship. Finally, there are his poems, and other works of art, sometimes famed everywhere and regarded as all but everlasting monuments; and they might always have been beneficent and tonic, but often are only hateful. The fictitious Adam of my eight stanzas has a speech precisely as pretty as his zealous author and patron could find for him, but the ruling imagination is that of a "wicked heart"; for this I regret to think that the real Adam, his maker, is responsible also.

Had we not better say that Adam was created half free, not wholly free? A theme which is not particularly explored in Scripture, but doubtless is there gratefully taken for granted, is that of the marvelous body created to house Adam's soul; replenishing, conditioning, repairing, preserving itself, almost without Adam's consciousness; a machine not of Adam's manufacture, but the fortress and security of his free enterprise. A tight and physical containment is appointed to the body; much of Adam's vital strength must be expended upon its secret operation, and it is just as well if it has not the freedom of Adam's imagination.

We come to Charles Coffin's account of Eve, and here I am all eyes and ears. ("Now my step quickens," says the Adam of my poem.) It appears that the agency in Eve's creation was Adam's as well as the Creator's. Adam took the initiative; he asked for it. Therefore it was from his body that the Creator got the rib out of which she was to be fashioned. This is not to say that the new creature was not as fully authorized as Adam. But she was a more separate and independent creature, says Dr. Coffin. God talks familiarly with Adam but not with Eve. Raphael talks at great length with Adam, but Eve after serving dinner stays discreetly in the background; and when he takes up the "abstruse" matter of the motions of the celestial universe she steals away to her flowers. Adam will explain all this to her later if she wishes. Clearly there is a deficiency in Eve's composition as compared with Adam's. She is not of the "intellectual" type, and it does not seem likely that she will be in all respects his congenial companion; there may have been some irony in the Creator's mind in complying with Adam's request.

Eve is freer than Adam in some respects, and is so declared by Dr. Coffin; she is more natural, confirmed in her direction already, therefore more spontaneous in her responses; she is less reflective. Her deficiency is in the freedom of those adventurous behaviors which go with rational discourse and the metaphysical imagination. So far as my eight stanzas are concerned, the matter turns on whether she is free to respond to the interests of her spouse as an artist; whose art this time is an extravagant "supposal" or fantasy, having a theological cast and an evil imagination. Is she capable of being swept off her feet by a work of art—especially one that invokes a vision of evil? Adam hopes to find her capable. But the answer is in the new stanzas. He concedes that she is not capable; he will not ask of her the impossible. She is less free than Adam. Speaking very roughly, let us say that she is one-quarter free.

I found these considerations somewhat chilling. But I asked myself: what development within Eve's personality was so uniquely important that it must replace the missing quarter of her freedom? The answer was not really difficult, and it could be checked against Scripture and Milton rather explicitly. Eve has a special function within her body, and for exercising it a virtue, a habit not acquired but already built into her unconscious mind. Behind it a quarter of her vital energy (if we have to quantify it) has been committed firmly to its consummation. She bears the children in her own body; then she cares for them, teaches them, defends them to the last extremity, even with her life if necessary. One of the most vivid of my memories comes back whenever I think of Eve's composition. It is the recollection of my first "tutorial" in my Oxford college. When I had read my appointed paper, there came the inst int suggestion, from the formidable philosopher who was my tutor, that I possess myself at once of *The Origin and Development of the Moral Ideas*, in two large volumes, published in 1906, by Edward Westermarck, professor of moral philosophy at the University of Finland, professor of sociology at the University of London. Two days later I was reading the chapter in which the "maternal instinct" is described as the origin of all human altruism. For the moral ideas of the male have to do with such motives as power, prestige, and aggressiveness. At once I reflected that no altruism is needed to motivate the conception of offspring; that is so important for family and tribe and history that in the scheme of creation the act was invested for both parties with a bodily pleasure so massive that it must prove more than ample for its occasions. The rearing of the children does not have such a sure sanction; unless it is the sanction of Eve's natural goodness, of the tender mercies which are sealed within her, awaiting with confidence their occasions.

This paragraph will carry a slightly rueful self-appraisal. Probably the most of my poems are about familiar and familial situations; domestic and homely things. Eventually I was surprised and rather set back by the sense of what a "bourgeois" poet they had turned me into. The "Prelude" seemed to promise a variation in my performance, but even here it is evident that I have reverted. The change of tune in the four new stanzas, and the abject capitulation of Adam, may cause me to be drummed out of the corps of smart and reputable poets; for surely within the whole circuit of poetic occasions I have descended to the nadir of available themes in order to occupy myself with—a baby-sitting. My pedestrian and precarious defense could only be the argument that in the degree of their commonplace such situations might be denoting precisely those patterns within the great Familial Configuration which had been ordained in our creation, and were therefore the ones likely to be standard and permanent.

Will my readers speculate and generalize with me a little? Suppose Eve first tempted Adam, whether or not instructed by a kindly Serpent as to the facts of life; for she would need to have a prescience of the sequel. She was successful; and perhaps she despised Adam a little for the innocence and haste with which he yielded. Then came the children. After this it would be Adam soliciting Eve; but if possible it would be on his own lordly conditions. Let her share his professional interests; then she will have his preoccupations, sometimes as evil as they will be good, but she will also have him; he may even suggest that less time should be spent with the children. But, even before Adam comes into her presence to make his proposition, he is condemned out of his own mouth. The children must occupy her mind now; they have replaced their father in her deepest affections; and if he desires her favors he will have to take them not on his terms but on hers, which will stipulate that he must share the responsibility for the children. I am aware that both Israel (which was responsible for the Old Testament) and Milton (who elaborated on its story) took a partisan view of Adam as the lord of the household. There has been much question of Milton's personal success in this role. But it was within the history of Israel, from the beginning to this day, that I could easily imagine that Adam's talent for the familial role had been altogether exceptional.

The tenth stanza continues the ninth, by providing a passage with erotic connotations, in order to display Adam truthfully; that requires its first three lines. The fourth line begins the denouement. Suddenly, as Adam approaches, he comes to his senses and knows that Eve will never accept his invitation; not the open and intellectual part, not the implicit erotic part if that is bound up with the other. He knows better than to say it to her actual person. Probably he will never say it out loud.

The twelfth stanza recalls a truancy of Adam's at some time or other, when he had gone among strangers trying to forget his Eve, whose feelings for him had not been the same after the coming of the children. He went on a journey. But what he found was that Eve was still the only woman for him. We respect his constancy.

In the last stanza Adam stands on the threshold of his house, but he stops a moment to fortify his wiser self against his own self-defeating eloquence. The final utterance of his soliloquy, and of the poem, is a two-line homage, half mystical, perhaps half maudlin, to the formidable yet beneficent dignity of her status and that of the children. We imagine that he is going to enjoy her favor, but his immediate motive is under the familial sign. He will sit with the children dutifully and, we will think, proudly. It is not the happiest ending that he could possibly conceive, but it is the best he had the right to expect.

Perhaps a kindly reader will wish him many happy returns of his homecoming. Does not the poem presuppose a crucial and habit-forming moment in his history? There will be many interims yet when he will be out in the free world again, busied in his own way professionally. But every time he takes his leave he will have said to them and himself: I shall return.

A Note About the Author

John Crowe Ransom

was born in Pulaski, Tennessee, in 1888. After attending Vanderbilt and Oxford (as a Rhodes scholar), he was a member of the faculty of Vanderbilt University from 1914 to 1937. He then taught at Kenyon College for twenty years and edited the *Kenyon Review*, which he founded in 1939. He has published more than a score of volumes of poetry and criticism, and has received the Bollingen Prize for Poetry, the Loines Memorial Fund Prize of the National Institute of Arts and Letters, the 1962 Fellowship Prize of the Academy of American Poets, and the National Book Award for Poetry for 1964. Mr. Ransom retired in 1958 and lived in Gambier, Ohio, until his death in 1974. Near the end of his life he wrote that "intellectually there has been no period of my life happier than this late one, where I am in the verse patch again."

A Note on the Type

This book was set in Monticello, a Linotype revival of the original Roman No. 1 cut by Archibald Binny and cast in 1796 by the Philadelphia type foundry Binny & Ronaldson. The face was named Monticello in honor of its use in the monumental fifty-volume *Papers of Thomas Jefferson*, published by Princeton University Press. Monticello is a transitional type design, embodying certain features of Bulmer and Baskerville, but it is a distinguished face in its own right.